SRA Reading Mastery

Signature Edition

Spelling Presentation Book
Grade 4

Robert Dixon
Siegfried Engelmann
Tina Wells

 SRA

Columbus, OH

SRAonline.com

 SRA

Copyright © 2008 by SRA/McGraw-Hill.

Printed in the United States of America.

Send all inquiries to this address:
SRA/McGraw-Hill
4400 Easton Commons
Columbus, OH 43219

ISBN: 978-0-07-612621-7
MHID: 0-07-612621-8

9 10 11 RMN 18 17 16

The *McGraw-Hill* Companies

Guide to *Spelling Presentation Book* Grade 4

Introduction

Present the spelling component of *Reading Mastery Signature Edition* Grade 4, at a time other than the period for reading. In other words, spelling lessons should not infringe upon the time scheduled for reading. Each spelling lesson takes about ten to fifteen minutes, so you can use these lessons flexibly during the time allotted for language arts instruction. Spelling instruction begins with lesson 1 of the reading program and goes with each reading lesson through 120. (You present spelling lesson 1 on the same day as reading lesson 1.) Remember, reading lessons match with spelling lessons, so under no circumstances should you end up on a spelling lesson beyond the reading lesson you are teaching.

Although these spelling lessons, when taught to mastery, will markedly improve students' spelling ability, their greatest value might be that of reinforcing reading. The ability to encode a word strengthens students' ability to decode a word.

Material

You present lessons from the Grade 4 *Spelling Presentation Book.* Your students write answers for some activities on their own paper. They will need a red pen on test day (every tenth lesson).

What Is Taught?

Three Approaches to Teaching Spelling Content
Reading Mastery Signature Edition, Grade 4 *Spelling* uses three approaches to teaching spelling content: whole-word, phonemic, and morphemic. Each approach has advantages and possible disadvantages. *Reading Mastery* Grade 4 *Spelling* combines all three approaches and is designed to maximize the advantages of each approach and minimize the disadvantages.

Whole Word

This approach requires students to memorize the spelling of individual words. Students are taught no rules but simply memorize information, such as "The word **quiet** is spelled **q-u-i-e-t.**"

The advantage of the whole-word approach is that it is the only way to teach words that do not fit generalizations, such as the word **answer.** The disadvantage of whole-word instruction is that it is inefficient. To teach two thousand words, each word must be presented as a separate entity, a rote unit that is essentially unrelated to other words being taught.

Phonemic

This approach, based on sound-symbol relationships, involves teaching students the letters for various sounds, such as "The sound /n/ is spelled with the letter **n.**"
The advantage of this approach is that it provides spellers with generalizations for spelling many words and word parts. This approach is most advantageous when applied to regular spelling words—those composed entirely of predictable, or stable, elements. For example, "The sound /m/ is spelled with the letter **m,** /a/ with **a,** and /n/ with **n. Man,** therefore, is spelled **m-a-n.**"

One problem with this approach, as it is traditionally used, is that it confuses reading objectives with spelling objectives. Many spellings produce the sound /ē/ (e-a, e-i, e-e, e, i-e). Reading instruction teaches learners what sound to say when presented with any of these symbols; however, the problem of spelling is different.

Students are presented with a sound in a word and must produce the appropriate spelling. Which spelling is correct? A tricky balance exists. The stable elements in a word like **teen** can be spelled by applying sound-symbol generalizations. At the same time, students must be taught to avoid the overgeneralization of spelling all long-e words with **e-e.**

The phonemic approach is weakest when applied to multisyllabic words, particularly those containing an unstressed vowel that sounds like "uh" and could be spelled with any vowel letter. The "uh" in the word relative (rel-uh-tiv) could be spelled with a, e, o, or u.

Morphemic

The morphemic approach to spelling teaches students to spell units—bases and affixes—of words and to put them together to form words. The term **morphograph** applies to all these units. A morphograph is the smallest word part that has meaning. For example, **water** is made of two syllables but only one morphograph.

The primary advantage of using morphographs is that a small number of them can be combined to form a large number of words. After students have learned some morphographs, spelling words composed of more than one morphograph is relatively easy.

Most morphographs are spelled the same way in every word in which they occur. Others, such as **hope,** change their spelling in some cases. But the change, such as dropping the final **e,** is predictable and can be taught through reliable spelling rules.

The morphemic approach is most efficient for multisyllabic words. These words typically defy phonemic analysis; however, they can be effectively taught as combinations of morphographs. Five or six hundred morphographs combine to form thousands of words.

One difficulty within a morphemic approach is that learning to spell morphographs may depend on sound-symbol and whole-word analyses.

The principal focus of *Reading Mastery, Grade 4 Spelling* is upon the *morphemic* approach to spelling. At this level, students have already learned phonemic spelling patterns. The morphemic emphasis of this level involves students learning numerous common prefixes and suffixes, word bases, and an introduction to non-word bases, such as **cept** in the word receptive. The program refers to such parts collectively as *morphographs.* Students add combinations of morphographs to one another in order to create new words, and they analyze the morphographs in whole, multi-morphograph words. Sometimes combining morphographs requires students to change the spelling of one or more parts. Rules govern such changes, which the program teaches to your students.

Reading Mastery Grade 4 *Spelling* also teaches students numerous irregularly spelled words, which are usually introduced in the context of sentences.

Whole Word

Sentences Many irregularly spelled words are introduced in sentences. Students master the spelling of irregular words within the model sentence, and then variations of the sentence are presented so that students apply the spelling of those words to various sentence contexts.

Whole Words

Sentence	Lesson Introduced
Whose turn is it to move?	42
Our yellow flowers bloomed early.	56
Carrying the heavy load is sure to make me breathe hard.	61
One athlete finished the contest before everyone else.	71
Our second surprise was especially exciting.	83
Nineteen athletes exercised throughout the morning.	92
People weren't interested in the photograph.	102
Anybody would rather be healthy instead of wealthy.	112

Morphemic

Prefixes and Suffixes Following is a list of lessons in which prefixes and suffixes are introduced.

Affixes

Prefix or Suffixes	Lesson Introduced
-ed	1
-est	1
-er	1
-ing	1
-s	1
re-	2
un-	3
-less	5
mis-	6
-ness	7
-able	8
pre-	12
-ly	(9), 13
-ful	(9), 15
-age	16
-al	17
-ish	18
-y	21
-es	27
-en	27
in-	29
con-	31
-ment	(45), 48
de-	49
ex-	62
pro-	81
-ive	82
-ion	87
-ous	96
-ure	107

Morphemic Principles and Rules The following is a list of lessons in which morphemic principles and rules are introduced. Preskills for these principles and rules are taught well in advance of the introduction of the principles and rules themselves.

Principles and Rules

Drop the final **e** from a word when the next morphograph begins with a vowel letter	7
Double the final consonant in a word that ends **cvc** when the next morphograph begins with a vowel letter	21
If **y** is at the end of a morphograph, then it is a vowel letter	22
We don't double **x** because the letter **x** acts like two consonant letters, **k** and **s**	32
Change the **y** to **i** when a word ends consonant-and-y, and the next next morphograph begins with anything, except **i**	34
Add **es** instead of **s** if a word ends in **s, x, sh, ch** Or in **x** Or in consonant-and-y	27 32 47
If **w** is at the end of a morphograph, then it is a vowel letter	41
A contraction is made from two words, and a contraction has a part missing	54
Double the final consonant in a word that ends q-u-VC when the next morphograph begins with a vowel letter	67
Business follows the y to i rule; **busyness** does not	63

Nonword Bases The following is a list of lessons in which nonword bases are introduced.

Nonword Bases

Base	Lesson Introduced	Example
tect	(108), 113	de**tect**ing
gress	(108), 114	pro**gress**
cept	(108), 115	re**cept**ive
ject	111	in**ject**ion

Assessment

You will administer a ten-word test on every tenth lesson, beginning with Lesson 10. Students will need a red pen.

How the Spelling Is Taught

Follow the same conventions and critical teaching practices for teaching the spelling lessons that you use for teaching the reading lessons. As in a reading lesson, utilize group responses, clear signals, and fast pacing.

Corrections

You will use a single basic correction procedure for correcting errors in the spelling lessons:

1. (Model.) Tell students the correct answer.
2. (Lead.) Say the response with students. You may need to repeat this step three to five times for all students to be firm.
3. (Test.) Check to make sure students respond correctly.
4. (Delayed test.) After students pass the test, return to the beginning of the exercise to determine if their response is firm.

Spelling Example
Students misspell a word in step *c* of the following example exercise.

Spelling Review

a. Get ready to spell words.
b. Word 1 is **thought.** Spell **thought.** Get ready. (Signal.) *T-H-O-U-G-H-T.*
c. Word 2 is **friend.** Spell **friend.** Get ready. (Signal.) *F-R-E-N-D.*

[Teacher corrects here.]

Correction:

(Stop as soon as a mistake occurs.)

1. (Model.) Listen: **F-R-I-E-N-D.**
2. (Lead.) With me. Spell **friend.** Get ready. (Signal and respond with students.) *F-R-I-E-N-D.*
3. (Test.) Your turn. Spell **friend.** Get ready. (Signal.) *F-R-I-E-N-D.*
4. (Delayed test) Spell **thought.** Get ready. (Signal.) *T-H-O-U-G-H-T.*
5. Spell friend again. Get ready. (Signal.) *F-R-I-E-N-D.*

If the error seems to be very minor—due perhaps to a lack of attention—use the same correction procedure without the "lead" step, which saves a little time. Note that the "delayed test" yields the most important diagnostic information. If your students have trouble on that step, start the basic correction procedure over and use the "lead" step three or more times. For the most difficult errors, multiple delayed tests are very effective. Use the correction procedure at other times during the lesson, during other lessons, while your students line up for recess, as students put up chairs and leave for the day, or any other time. This shows students that you think it is important for them to learn the difficult word, but moreover, gives them multiple opportunities, spread over time, to remember the correct spelling.

Sentence Repetition Example
Students make an error repeating a sentence exactly.

Sentence Variation

a. Get ready to write on lined paper.

• You are going to write a sentence made up of words you know how to spell. Put the right end mark at the end of the sentence.

b. The sentence is: **We excitedly exchanged great friendship.**

• Say that sentence. Get ready. (Signal.) *We excited...*

Correction:

(Stop as soon as a mistake occurs.)

1. (Model.) Listen: **We excitedly exchanged great friendship.**

2. (Lead.) With me. Say that sentence. Get ready. (Signal and respond with students.) *We excitedly exchanged great friendship.*

3. (Test.) Your turn. Say that sentence. Get ready. (Signal.) *We excitedly exchanged great friendship.*

4. (Delayed test.) Again. Say that sentence. Get ready. (Signal.) *We excitedly exchanged great friendship.*

LESSON 1

EXERCISE 1

Affixes

a. You're going to write words on lined paper. Number your paper from 1 through 5. ✔

b. Word 1 is **clean.** What word? (Signal.) *Clean.*
- Write the word **clean.** ✔

c. Word 2 is **print.** What word? (Signal.) *Print.*
- Write the word **print.** ✔

d. Word 3 is **farm.** What word? (Signal.) *Farm.*
- Write the word **farm.** ✔

e. Word 4 is **camp.** What word? (Signal.) *Camp.*
- Write the word **camp.** ✔

f. Word 5 is **jump.** What word? (Signal.) *Jump.*
- Write the word **jump.** ✔

g. (Write on the board:)

> 1. clean + er =
> 2. print + ed =
> 3. farm + er =
> 4. camp + ing =
> 5. jump + s =

- Now you're going to add suffixes to these words.

h. After **clean** write a plus mark and **e-r.** ✔ After **e-r** write an equal sign. ✔

i. Write the plus signs, suffixes, and equal signs shown for the rest of the words. ✔

j. You're going to add the suffixes to make new words.

k. Word 1 is **cleaner.** What word? (Signal.) *Cleaner.*
- Write the word **cleaner** after the equal sign. ✔
- (Write to show:)

> 1. clean + er = cleaner

- Here's what you should have: **clean** plus **e-r** equals **cleaner.**

l. Word 2 is **printed.** What word? (Signal.) *Printed.*
- Write the word **printed** after the equal sign. ✔

m. Word 3 is **farmer.** What word? (Signal.) *Farmer.*
- Write the word **farmer** after the equal sign. ✔

n. Word 4 is **camping.** What word? (Signal.) *Camping.*
- Write the word **camping** after the equal sign. ✔

o. Word 5 is **jumps.** What word? (Signal.) *Jumps.*
- Write the word **jumps** after the equal sign. ✔

p. Check your work. Make an **X** next to any word you got wrong.

q. Word 1. Spell **cleaner.** Get ready. (Tap for each letter.) *C-L-E-A-N-E-R.*
- (Repeat for: **2. printed, 3. farmer, 4. camping, 5. jumps.**)

EXERCISE 2

Word Introduction

a. (Write on the board:)

> wander
> listen
> search
> build
> view
> sort

b. Get ready to read these words.
- First word: **wander.** What word? (Signal.) *Wander.*

c. Next word: **listen.** What word? (Signal.) *Listen.*
- (Repeat for: **search, build, view, sort.**)

d. Now spell those words.
- Spell **wander.** Get ready. (Signal.) *W-A-N-D-E-R.*

e. Spell **listen.** Get ready. (Signal.) *L-I-S-T-E-N.*
- (Repeat for: **search, build, view, sort.**)

f. (Erase the board.)
- Spell the words without looking.

g. Spell **wander.** Get ready. (Signal.) *W-A-N-D-E-R.*

h. Spell **listen.** Get ready. (Signal.) *L-I-S-T-E-N.*
- (Repeat for: **search, build, view, sort.**)

i. Get ready to write those words.
j. Word 1: **wander.** Write it. ✔
• (Repeat for: **2. listen, 3. search, 4. build, 5. view, 6. sort.**)

EXERCISE 3

Morphograph Introduction

a. (Write on the board:)

> 1. unclaimed = un + claim + ed
>
> 2. unpacking = un + pack + ing
>
> 3. helper = help + er

b. Prefixes, suffixes, and base words can all be called **morphographs.**
c. What can you call all prefixes, suffixes, and base words? (Signal.) *Morphographs.*
• (Repeat until firm.)
d. The first **morphograph** in **unclaimed** is **un.**
• The next **morphograph** in **unclaimed** is **claim.**
• The next **morphograph** in **unclaimed** is **e-d.**

e. Look at word 2. ✔
• What's the first **morphograph** in **unpacking?** (Signal.) *Un.*
• What's the next **morphograph** in **unpacking?** (Signal.) *Pack.*
• What's the next **morphograph** in **unpacking?** (Signal.) *Ing.*
f. Look at word 3. ✔
• What's the first **morphograph** in **helper?** (Signal.) *Help.*
• What's the next **morphograph** in **helper?** (Signal.) *Er.*
g. (Give individual turns on identifying the morphographs in: **1. unclaimed, 2. unpacking, 3. helper.**)

LESSON 2

EXERCISE 1

Affix Introduction

a. (Write on the board:)

> 1. re + build =
> 2. re + hire =
> 3. re + tell =

b. In these words, the prefix **re** means: **again.**
- What does **re** mean? (Signal.) *Again.*

c. So what word means **build again?** (Signal.) *Rebuild.*
- What word means **hire again?** (Signal.) *Rehire.*
- What word means **tell again?** (Signal.) *Retell.*

d. Number your paper from 1 to 3. ✔
- Add **re** to the first word from the board to make a new word. Write just the new word. ✔
- (Write on the board:)

> 1. rebuild

- Here's what you should have.

e. Add the morphograph **re** to make new words 2 and 3. ✔

f. Check your work. Make an **X** next to any word you got wrong.

g. Word 1. Spell **rebuild.** Get ready. (Tap for each letter.) *R-E-B-U-I-L-D.*
- (Repeat for: **2. rehire, 3. retell.**)

EXERCISE 2

Word Introduction

a. (Write on the board:)

> straight
> light
> equal
> cheap
> sleep
> quote

b. Get ready to read these words.
- First word: **straight.** What word? (Signal.) *Straight.*

c. Next word: **light.** What word? (Signal.) *Light.*
- (Repeat for: **equal, cheap, sleep, quote.**)

d. Now spell those words.
- Spell **straight.** Get ready. (Signal.) *S-T-R-A-I-G-H-T.*

e. Spell **light.** Get ready. (Signal.) *L-I-G-H-T.*
- (Repeat for: **equal, cheap, sleep, quote.**)

f. (Erase the board.)
- Spell the words without looking.

g. Spell **straight.** Get ready. (Signal.) *S-T-R-A-I-G-H-T.*

h. Spell **light.** Get ready. (Signal.) *L-I-G-H-T.*
- (Repeat for: **equal, cheap, sleep, quote.**)

i. Get ready to write those words.

j. Word 1: **straight.** Write it. ✔
- (Repeat for: **2. quote 3. equal, 4. cheap, 5. sleep, 6. light.**)

EXERCISE 3

Prompted Review

a. (Write on the board:)

> 1. listen
> 2. view
> 3. build
> 4. cleaner
> 5. wander
> 6. search

b. Word 1 is **listen.** Spell **listen.** Get ready. (Signal.) *L-I-S-T-E-N.*

c. Word 2 is **view.** Spell **view.** Get ready. (Signal.) *V-I-E-W.*

d. (Repeat step c for: **3. build, 4. cleaner, 5. wander, 6. search.**)

e. (Erase the board.)
- Now spell those words without looking.

f. Word 1 is **listen.** Spell **listen.** Get ready. (Signal.) *L-I-S-T-E-N.*

g. Word 2 is **view.** Spell **view.** Get ready. (Signal.) *V-I-E-W.*

h. (Repeat step g for: **3. build, 4. cleaner, 5. wander, 6. search.**)

i. (Give individual turns on **1. listen, 2. view, 3. build, 4. cleaner, 5. wander, 6. search.**)

EXERCISE 1

Affix Introduction

a. (Write on the board:)

> 1. un + like =
> 2. un + even =
> 3. un + clear =

• In these words, the prefix **un** means: **not.**

b. What does **un** mean? (Signal.) *Not.*

c. So what word means **not like?** (Signal.) *Unlike.*

• What word means **not even?** (Signal.) *Uneven.*

• What word means **not clear?** (Signal.) *Unclear.*

d. Number your paper from 1 to 3. ✔

e. Add the morphograph **un.** Write just the new words. ✔

f. Check your work. Make an **X** next to any word you got wrong.

g. Word 1. Spell **unlike.** Get ready. (Tap for each letter.) *U-N-L-I-K-E.*

• (Repeat for: **2. uneven, 3. unclear.**)

EXERCISE 2

Word Introduction

a. (Write on the board:)

> stretch
> child
> care
> cloud
> spell
> source

b. Get ready to read these words.

• First word: **stretch.** What word? (Signal.) *Stretch.*

c. Next word: **child.** What word? (Signal.) *Child.*

• (Repeat for: **care, cloud, spell, source.**)

d. Now spell those words.

• Spell **stretch.** Get ready. (Signal.) *S-T-R-E-T-C-H.*

e. Spell **child.** Get ready. (Signal.) *C-H-I-L-D.*

• (Repeat for: **care, cloud, spell, source.**)

f. (Erase the board.)

• Spell the words without looking.

g. Spell **stretch.** Get ready. (Signal.) *S-T-R-E-T-C-H.*

h. Spell **child.** Get ready. (Signal.) *C-H-I-L-D.*

• (Repeat for: **care, cloud, spell, source.**)

i. Get ready to write those words.

j. First word: **cloud.** Write it. ✔

• (Repeat for: **child, care, stretch, spell, source.**)

EXERCISE 3

Prompted Review

a. (Write on the board:)

> 1. rebuild
> 2. straight
> 3. listen
> 4. equal
> 5. cheap
> 6. light

b. Word 1 is **rebuild.** Spell **rebuild.** Get ready. (Signal.) *R-E-B-U-I-L-D.*

c. Word 2 is **straight.** Spell **straight.** Get ready. (Signal.) *S-T-R-A-I-G-H-T.*

d. (Repeat step c for: **3. listen, 4. equal, 5. cheap, 6. light.**)

e. (Erase the board.)

• Now spell those words without looking.

f. Word 1 is **rebuild.** Spell **rebuild.** Get ready. (Signal.) *R-E-B-U-I-L-D.*

g. Word 2 is **straight.** Spell **straight.** Get ready. (Signal.) *S-T-R-A-I-G-H-T.*

h. (Repeat step g for: **3. listen, 4. equal, 5. cheap, 6. light.**)

i. (Give individual turns on **1. rebuild, 2. straight, 3. listen, 4. equal, 5. cheap, 6. light.**)

LESSON 4

EXERCISE 1

Morphograph Introduction

a. (Write on the board:)

> 1. rebuilding = re + build + ing
>
> 2. unclear = un + clear
>
> 3. reprinted = re + print + ed

b. Prefixes, suffixes, and base words can all be called **morphographs.**

c. What can you call all prefixes, suffixes, and base words? (Signal.) *Morphographs.*
- (Repeat until firm.)

d. The first **morphograph** in **rebuilding** is **re.**
- The next **morphograph** in **rebuilding** is **build.**
- The next **morphograph** in **rebuilding** is **ing.**

e. Look at word 2. ✔
- What's the first **morphograph** in **unclear?** (Signal.) *Un.*
- What's the next **morphograph** in **unclear?** (Signal.) *Clear.*

f. Look at word 3. ✔
- What's the first **morphograph** in **reprinted?** (Signal.) *Re.*
- What's the next **morphograph** in **reprinted?** (Signal.) *Print.*
- What's the next **morphograph** in **reprinted?** (Signal.) *E-D.*

g. (Give individual turns on identifying the morphographs in: **1. rebuilding, 2. unclear, 3. reprinted.**)

EXERCISE 2

Word Introduction

a. (Write on the board:)

> happy
> lock
> study
> glory
> sign
> people

b. Get ready to read these words.
- First word: **happy.** What word? (Signal.) *Happy.*

c. Next word: **lock.** What word? (Signal.) *Lock.*
- (Repeat for: **study, glory, sign, people.**)

d. Now spell those words.
- Spell **happy.** Get ready. (Signal.) *H-A-P-P-Y.*

e. Spell **lock.** Get ready. (Signal.) *L-O-C-K.*
- (Repeat for: **study, glory, sign, people.**)

f. (Erase the board.)
- Spell the words without looking.

g. Spell **happy.** Get ready. (Signal.) *H-A-P-P-Y.*

h. Spell **lock.** Get ready. (Signal.) *L-O-C-K.*
- (Repeat for: **study, glory, sign, people.**)

i. Get ready to write those words.

j. Word 1: **study.** Write it. ✔
- (Repeat for: **2. sign, 3. happy, 4. glory, 5. lock, 6. people.**)

EXERCISE 3

Prompted Review

a. (Write on the board:)

> 1. source
> 2. unclear
> 3. straight
> 4. listen
> 5. search
> 6. stretch

b. Word 1 is **source.** Spell **source.** Get ready. (Signal.) *S-O-U-R-C-E.*

c. Word 2 is **unclear.** Spell **unclear.** Get ready. (Signal.) *U-N-C-L-E-A-R.*

d. (Repeat step c for: **3. straight, 4. listen, 5. search, 6. stretch.**)

e. (Erase the board.)
- Now spell those words without looking.

f. Word 1 is **source.** Spell **source.** Get ready. (Signal.) *S-O-U-R-C-E.*

g. Word 2 is **unclear.** Spell **unclear.** Get ready. (Signal.) *U-N-C-L-E-A-R.*

h. (Repeat step g for: **3. straight, 4. listen, 5. search, 6. stretch.**)

i. (Give individual turns on **1. source, 2. unclear, 3. straight, 4. listen, 5. search, 6. stretch.**)

EXERCISE 1

Affix Introduction

a. (Write on the board:)

> 1. help + less =
> 2. child + less =
> 3. cloud + less =

- All these words have the morphograph **less.**
b. Number your paper from 1 to 3. ✔
c. Add the morphographs together. Write just the new words. ✔
d. Check your work. Make an **X** next to any word you got wrong.
e. Word 1. Spell **helpless.** Get ready. (Tap for each letter.) *H-E-L-P-L-E-S-S.*
- (Repeat for: **2. childless, 3. cloudless.**)

EXERCISE 2

Vowels and Consonants

a. (Write on the board:)

> 1. r a n c h   3. s c r u b
>
> 2. p l a n   4. p r i n t

- Copy the words. Skip a line between each word. Raise your hand when you're finished. ✔
b. You're going to write **c** or **v** above each letter of the words. You'll write **c** above the consonants and **v** above the vowels.
- Everybody, what will you write above the consonants? (Signal.) *C.*
- What will you write above the vowels? (Signal.) *V.*
- Tell me the vowel letters. Get ready. (Signal.) *A, E, I, O, U.*
c. Write **c** or **v** above each letter in the word **ranch.** Raise your hand when you're finished.
(Observe students and give feedback.)
- (Write to show:)

> c v c c c
> 1. r a n c h

- Check your work. Here's what you should have. Make an **X** next to the word **ranch** if you got it wrong. ✔
d. Do the rest of the words. Write **c** or **v** above each letter. Raise your hand when you're finished.
(Observe students and give feedback.)
e. (Write to show:)

> c v c c c   c c c v c
> 1. r a n c h   3. s c r u b
>
> c c v c   c c v c c
> 2. p l a n   4. p r i n t

- Check your work. Here's what you should have. Make an **X** next to any word you got wrong. ✔

EXERCISE 3

Spelling Review

a. You're going to spell words.
b. Word 1 is **listen.** Spell **listen.** Get ready. (Signal.) *L-I-S-T-E-N.*
c. Word 2 is **straight.** Spell **straight.** Get ready. (Signal.) *S-T-R-A-I-G-H-T.*
d. Word 3 is **source.** Spell **source.** Get ready. (Signal.) *S-O-U-R-C-E.*
e. Word 4 is **stretch.** Spell **stretch.** Get ready. (Signal.) *S-T-R-E-T-C-H.*
f. Word 5 is **sign.** Spell **sign.** Get ready. (Signal.) *S-I-G-N.*
g. Word 6 is **equal.** Spell **equal.** Get ready. (Signal.) *E-Q-U-A-L.*
h. Word 7 is **people.** Spell **people.** Get ready. (Signal.) *P-E-O-P-L-E.*
i. Word 8 is **search.** Spell **search.** Get ready. (Signal.) *S-E-A-R-C-H.*
j. (Give individual turns on: **1. listen, 2. straight, 3. source, 4. stretch, 5. sign, 6. equal, 7. people, 8. search.**)

LESSON 6

EXERCISE 1

Affix Introduction

a. (Write on the board:)

> 1. mis + spell =
> 2. mis + quote =
> 3. mis + take =

- All these words have the morphograph **mis.**
b. Number your paper from 1 to 3. ✔
c. Add the morphographs together. Write just the new words. ✔
d. Check your work. Make an **X** next to any word you got wrong.
e. Word 1. Spell **misspell.** Get ready. (Tap for each letter.) *M-I-S-S-P-E-L-L.*
- (Repeat for: **2. misquote, 3. mistake.**)

EXERCISE 2

Vowels and Consonants

a. (Write on the board:)

> 1. child   3. lock
>
> 2. care   4. sign

- Copy the words. Skip a line between each word. Raise your hand when you're finished. ✔
b. You're going to write **c** or **v** above each letter of the words. You'll write **c** above the consonants and **v** above the vowels.
c. Do the words on your own. Write **c** or **v** above each letter. Raise your hand when you're finished.
(Observe students and give feedback.)
d. (Write to show:)

> ```
>     c c v c c      c v c c
> 1. child       3. lock
>     c v c v        c v c c
> 2. care        4. sign
> ```

- Check your work. Here's what you should have. Make an **X** next to any word you got wrong. ✔

EXERCISE 3

Morphographic Analysis

a. (Write on the board:)

> 1. cloudless = _____
>
> 2. reviewing = _____
>
> 3. misspelled = _____
>
> 4. helpless = _____

- Number your paper from 1 to 4. ✔
- These words are made up of more than one morphograph. You're going to write the morphographs that go in each blank.
b. **Cloudless.** What's the first morphograph in **cloudless?** (Signal.) *Cloud.*
- Item 1. Write **cloud** and a plus sign. ✔
c. What's the next morphograph in **cloudless?** (Signal.) *Less.*
- Write **less.** ✔
d. (Write to show:)

> 1. cloudless = cloud + less

- Raise your hand if you wrote **cloud** plus **less.** ✔
e. Do the rest of the words on your own. ✔
f. (Write to show:)

> 1. cloudless = cloud + less
>
> 2. reviewing = re + view + ing
>
> 3. misspelled = mis + spell + ed
>
> 4. helpless = help + less

- Check your work. Make an **X** next to any item you got wrong. ✔

EXERCISE 1

Affix Introduction

a. (Write on the board:)

> 1. dark + ness =
> 2. quiet + ness =
> 3. bold + ness =

- All these words have the morphograph **ness.**
b. Number your paper from 1 to 3. ✔
c. Add the morphographs together. Write just the new words. ✔
d. Check your work. Make an **X** next to any word you got wrong.
e. Word 1. Spell **darkness.** Get ready. (Tap for each letter.) *D-A-R-K-N-E-S-S.*
- (Repeat for: **2. quietness, 3. boldness.**)

EXERCISE 2

Word Introduction

a. (Write on the board:)

> quiet
> fight
> break
> port
> school
> author

b. Get ready to read these words.
- First word: **quiet.** What word? (Signal.) *Quiet.*
c. Next word: **fight.** What word? (Signal.) *Fight.*
- (Repeat for: **break, port, school, author.**)
d. Now spell those words.
- Spell **quiet.** Get ready. (Signal.) *Q-U-I-E-T.*
e. Spell **fight.** Get ready. (Signal.) *F-I-G-H-T.*
- (Repeat for: **break, port, school, author.**)
f. (Erase the board.)
- Spell the words without looking.
g. Spell **quiet.** Get ready. (Signal.) *Q-U-I-E-T.*
h. Spell **fight.** Get ready. (Signal.) *F-I-G-H-T.*
- (Repeat for: **break, port, school, author.**)

EXERCISE 3

Final e Words

a. (Write on the board:)

> hope + ing =
>
> hope + less =

b. When we add a morphograph to a word that ends with **e,** we sometimes have to change the spelling of that word.
- Here is the rule: Drop the **e** from the word when the next morphograph begins with a vowel letter.
c. (Point to **ing** on the board.)
- Does this morphograph begin with a vowel letter or a consonant letter? (Signal.) *A vowel letter.*
- (Write to show:)

> v
> hope + ing =
>
> hope + less =

d. The morphograph **ing** begins with a vowel letter, so we have to drop the **e** from **hope** when we add **ing.**
- (Write to show:)

> v
> hope + ing = hoping
>
> hope + less =

e. (Point to **less** on the board.)
- Does this morphograph begin with a vowel letter or a consonant letter? (Signal.) *A consonant letter.*
- (Write to show:)

> v
> hope + ing = hoping
> c
> hope + less =

f. The morphograph **less** does not begin with a vowel letter, so we don't have to drop the **e** from **hope** when we add **less.**

• (Write to show:)

>   **v**
> **hope + ing = hoping**
>   **c**
> **hope + less = hopeless**

g. Everyone, spell **hoping.** Get ready. (Signal.) *H-O-P-I-N-G.*

h. Now spell **hopeless.** Get ready. (Signal.) *H-O-P-E-L-E-S-S.*

EXERCISE 1

Affix Introduction

a. (Write on the board:)

> 1. wash + able =
> 2. port + able =
> 3. stretch + able =

*   All these words have the morphograph **able.**
b. Number your paper from 1 to 3. ✔
c. Add the morphographs together. Write just the new words. ✔
d. Check your work. Make an **X** next to any word you got wrong.
e. Word 1. Spell **washable.** Get ready. (Tap for each letter.) *W-A-S-H-A-B-L-E.*
*   (Repeat for: **2. portable, 3. stretchable.**)

EXERCISE 2

Word Introduction

a. (Write on the board:)

> caught
> picture
> together
> wrong

b. Get ready to read these words.
*   First word: **caught.** What word? (Signal.) *Caught.*
c. Next word: **picture.** What word? (Signal.) *Picture.*
*   (Repeat for: **together, wrong.**)
d. Now spell those words.
*   Spell **caught.** Get ready. (Signal.) *C-A-U-G-H-T.*
e. Spell **picture.** Get ready. (Signal.) *P-I-C-T-U-R-E.*
*   (Repeat for: **together, wrong.**)
f. (Erase the board.)
*   Spell the words without looking.
g. Spell **caught.** Get ready. (Signal.) *C-A-U-G-H-T.*
h. Spell **picture.** Get ready. (Signal.) *P-I-C-T-U-R-E.*
*   (Repeat for: **together, wrong.**)

EXERCISE 3

Final e Words

a. (Write on the board:)

> like + ness =
>
> like + able =

b. When we add a morphograph to a word that ends with **e,** we sometimes have to change the spelling of that word.
*   Here is the rule: Drop the **e** from the word when the next morphograph begins with a vowel letter.
c. (Point to **ness** on the board.)
*   Does this morphograph begin with a vowel letter or a consonant letter? (Signal.) *A consonant letter.*
*   (Write to show:)

>   c
> like + ness =
>
> like + able =

d. The morphograph **ness** begins with a consonant letter, so we don't have to drop the **e** from **like** when we add **ness.**
*   (Write to show:)

>   c
> like + ness = likeness
>
> like + able =

e. (Point to **able** on the board.)
*   Does this morphograph begin with a vowel letter or a consonant letter? (Signal.) *A vowel letter.*
*   (Write to show:)

>   c
> like + ness = likeness
>   v
> like + able =

f. The morphograph **able** does begin with a vowel letter, so we have to drop the **e** from **like** when we add **able.**

• (Write to show:)

> c
> **like + ness = likeness**
> v
> **like + able = likable**

g. Everyone, spell **likeness.** Get ready. (Signal.) *L-I-K-E-N-E-S-S.*

h. Now spell **likable.** Get ready. (Signal.) *L-I-K-A-B-L-E.*

LESSON 9

EXERCISE 1

Word Introduction

a. (Write on the board:)

> might
> story
> style
> voice
> choice

b. Get ready to read these words.
- First word: **might.** What word? (Signal.) *Might.*
c. Next word: **story.** What word? (Signal.) *Story.*
- (Repeat for: **style, voice, choice.**)
d. Now spell those words.
- Spell **might.** Get ready. (Signal.) *M-I-G-H-T.*
e. Spell **story.** Get ready. (Signal.) *S-T-O-R-Y.*
- (Repeat for: **style, voice, choice.**)
f. (Erase the board.)
- Spell the words without looking.
g. Spell **might.** Get ready. (Signal.) *M-I-G-H-T.*
h. Spell **story.** Get ready. (Signal.) *S-T-O-R-Y.*
- (Repeat for: **style, voice, choice.**)
i. Get ready to write those words.
j. Word 1: **voice.** Write it. ✔
- (Repeat for: **2. style, 3. story, 4. might, 5. choice.**)

EXERCISE 2

Final e Rule

a. (Write on the board:)

> 1. sure + ness =
>
> 2. sad + ly =
>
> 3. ride + ing =
>
> 4. glide + er =
>
> 5. wish + ful =

b. Number your paper from 1 through 5. ✔ Write these morphographs on your paper with the plus and equal signs. ✔
c. When do you drop the **e** from a word? (Signal.) *When the next morphograph begins with a vowel letter.*
d. Do these words on your own. Some of these words follow the final **e** rule. ✔
e. Check your work. Make an **X** next to any word you got wrong.
f. Word 1. Spell **sureness.** Get ready. (Tap for each letter.) *S-U-R-E-N-E-S-S.*
- (Repeat for: **2. sadly, 3. riding, 4. glider, 5. wishful.**)

EXERCISE 3

Prompted Review

a. (Write on the board:)

> 1. another
> 2. caught
> 3. together
> 4. washable
> 5. school
> 6. wrong
> 7. author
> 8. sign

b. Word 1 is **another.** Spell **another.** Get ready. (Signal.) *A-N-O-T-H-E-R.*
c. Word 2 is **caught.** Spell **caught.** Get ready. (Signal.) *C-A-U-G-H-T.*
d. (Repeat step c for: **3. together, 4. washable, 5. school, 6. wrong, 7. author, 8. sign.**)
e. (Erase the board.)
- Now spell those words without looking.
f. Word 1 is **another.** Spell **another.** Get ready. (Signal.) *A-N-O-T-H-E-R.*
g. Word 2 is **caught.** Spell **caught.** Get ready. (Signal.) *C-A-U-G-H-T.*
h. (Repeat step g for: **3. together, 4. washable, 5. school, 6. wrong, 7. author, 8. sign.**)
i. (Give individual turns on **1. another, 2. caught, 3. together, 4. washable, 5. school, 6. wrong, 7. author, 8. sign.**)

EXERCISE 1

> *Note:* In step **e** students will need a red pen (or colored pencil).

Test

a. Today you have a spelling test. Number your lined paper from 1 through 10. ✔

b. Word 1 is **rebuild.** What word? (Signal.) *Rebuild.*

- Write the word **rebuild.** ✔

c. Word 2 is **straight.** What word? (Signal.) *Straight.*

- Write the word **straight.** ✔

d. (Repeat step *c* for: **3. helpless, 4. together, 5. school, 6. wrong, 7. equal, 8. stretch, 9. sign, 10. wander.**)

e. Pick up your red pen. ✔
Make an **X** next to any word you spelled wrong.

- (Write on the board:)

1. rebuild	6. wrong
2. straight	7. equal
3. helpless	8. stretch
4. together	9. sign
5. school	10. wander

- Write the correct spelling next to any word you spelled wrong.
(Observe students and give feedback.)

Word Introduction

a. (Write on the board:)

> thought
> world
> serve
> grudge
> charge

b. Get ready to read these words.
- First word: **thought.** What word? (Signal.) *Thought.*

c. Next word: **world.** What word? (Signal.) *World.*
- (Repeat for: **serve, grudge, charge.**)

d. Now spell those words.
- Spell **thought.** Get ready. (Signal.) *T-H-O-U-G-H-T.*

e. Spell **world.** Get ready. (Signal.) *W-O-R-L-D.*
- (Repeat for: **serve, grudge, charge.**)

f. (Erase the board.)
- Spell the words without looking.

g. Spell **thought.** Get ready. (Signal.) *T-H-O-U-G-H-T.*

h. Spell **world.** Get ready. (Signal.) *W-O-R-L-D.*
- (Repeat for: **serve, grudge, charge.**)

Final e Rule

a. (Write on the board:)

> 1. fine + ness =
>
> 2. serve + ing =
>
> 3. move + able =
>
> 4. spell + ing =
>
> 5. care + ing =

b. Number your paper from 1 through 5. ✔
Write these words and suffixes on your paper with the plus and equal signs. ✔

c. When do you drop the **e** from a word? (Signal.) *When the next morphograph begins with a vowel letter.*

d. Do these words on your own. Some of these words follow the final **e** rule. ✔

e. Check your work. Make an **X** next to any word you got wrong.

f. Word 1. Spell **fineness.** Get ready. (Tap for each letter.) *F-I-N-E-N-E-S-S.*
- (Repeat for: **2. serving, 3. movable, 4. spelling, 5. caring.**)

Prompted Review

a. (Write on the board:)

> 1. style
> 2. together
> 3. school
> 4. story
> 5. choice

b. Word 1 is **style.** Spell **style.** Get ready. (Signal.) *S-T-Y-L-E.*

c. Word 2 is **together.** Spell **together.** Get ready. (Signal.) *T-O-G-E-T-H-E-R.*

d. (Repeat step c for: **3. school, 4. story, 5. choice.**)

e. (Erase the board.)
- Now spell those words without looking.

f. Word 1 is **style.** Spell **style.** Get ready. (Signal.) *S-T-Y-L-E.*

g. Word 2 is **together.** Spell **together.** Get ready. (Signal.) *T-O-G-E-T-H-E-R.*

h. (Repeat step g for: **3. school, 4. story, 5. choice.**)

i. (Give individual turns on **1. style, 2. together, 3. school, 4. story, 5. choice.**)

LESSON 12

EXERCISE 1

Word Introduction

a. (Write on the board:)

> busy
> noise
> sketch
> twice
> bench

b. Get ready to read these words.
- First word: **busy.** What word? (Signal.) *Busy.*
c. Next word: **noise.** What word? (Signal.) *Noise.*
- (Repeat for: **sketch, twice, bench.**)
d. Now spell those words.
- Spell **busy.** Get ready. (Signal.) *B-U-S-Y.*
e. Spell **noise.** Get ready. (Signal.) *N-O-I-S-E.*
- (Repeat for: **sketch, twice, bench.**)
f. (Erase the board.)

- Spell the words without looking.
g. Spell **busy.** Get ready. (Signal.) *B-U-S-Y.*
h. Spell **noise.** Get ready. (Signal.) *N-O-I-S-E.*
- (Repeat for: **sketch, twice, bench.**)
i. Get ready to write those words.
j. Word 1: **twice.** Write it. ✔
- (Repeat for: **2. bench, 3. sketch, 4. busy, 5. noise.**)

EXERCISE 2

Affix Introduction

a. (Write on the board:)

> 1. pre + view =
> 2. pre + wash =
> 3. pre + sent =

- All these words have the morphograph **pre.**
b. Number your paper from 1–3. ✔
c. Add the morphographs together. Write just the new words. ✔
d. Check your work. Make an **X** next to any word you got wrong.
e. Word 1. Spell **preview.** Get ready. (Tap for each letter.) *P-R-E-V-I-E-W.*
- (Repeat for: **2. prewash, 3. present.**)

EXERCISE 3

Prompted Review

a. (Write on the board:)

> 1. charging
> 2. curable
> 3. careless
> 4. thought
> 5. recharge

b. Word 1 is **charging.** Spell **charging.** Get ready. (Signal.) *C-H-A-R-G-I-N-G.*
c. Word 2 is **curable.** Spell **curable.** Get ready. (Signal.) *C-U-R-A-B-L-E.*
d. (Repeat step c for: **3. careless, 4. thought, 5. recharge.**)
e. (Erase the board.)

- Now spell those words without looking.
f. Word 1 is **charging.** Spell **charging.** Get ready. (Signal.) *C-H-A-R-G-I-N-G.*
g. Word 2 is **curable.** Spell **curable.** Get ready. (Signal.) *C-U-R-A-B-L-E.*
h. (Repeat step g for: **3. careless, 4. thought, 5. recharge.**)
i. (Give individual turns on **1. charging, 2. curable, 3. careless, 4. thought, 5. recharge.**)

EXERCISE 1

Word Introduction

a. (Write on the board:)

> chalk
> several
> person
> wreck
> note

b. Get ready to read these words.
- First word: **chalk.** What word? (Signal.) *Chalk.*
c. Next word: **several.** What word? (Signal.) *Several.*
- (Repeat for: **person, wreck, note.**)
d. Now spell those words.
- Spell **chalk.** Get ready. (Signal.) *C-H-A-L-K.*
e. Spell **several.** Get ready. (Signal.) *S-E-V-E-R-A-L.*
- (Repeat for: **person, wreck, note.**)
f. (Erase the board.)
- Spell the words without looking.
g. Spell **chalk.** Get ready. (Signal.) *C-H-A-L-K.*
h. Spell **several.** Get ready. (Signal.) *S-E-V-E-R-A-L.*
- (Repeat for: **person, wreck, note.**)

EXERCISE 2

Affix Introduction

a. (Write on the board:)

> 1. quiet + ly =
> 2. cold + ly =
> 3. light + ly =

- All these words have the morphograph **ly.**
b. Number your paper from 1 to 3. ✔
c. Add the morphographs together. Write just the new words. ✔
d. Check your work. Make an **X** next to any word you got wrong.
e. Word 1. Spell **quietly.** Get ready. (Tap for each letter.) *Q-U-I-E-T-L-Y.*
- (Repeat for: **2. coldly, 3. lightly.**)

EXERCISE 3

Morphographic Analysis

a. (Write on the board:)

> 1. presented = _____
> 2. unstretchable = _____
> 3. careless = _____
> 4. resigning = _____
> 5. unclearest = _____
> 6. helplessness = _____

- Number your paper from 1 to 6. ✔
- These words are made up of more than one morphograph. You're going to write the morphographs that go in each blank.
b. **Presented.** What's the first morphograph in **presented?** (Signal.) *Pre.*
- Item 1. Write **pre** and a plus sign. ✔
c. What's the next morphograph in **presented?** (Signal.) *Sent.*
- Write **sent** and a plus sign.
d. What's the next morphograph in **presented?** (Signal.) *E-D.*
- Write **e-d.** ✔
e. (Write to show:)

> 1. presented = pre + sent + ed

- Raise your hand if you wrote **pre** plus **sent** plus **e-d.** ✔
f. Do the rest of the words on your own. ✔
g. (Write to show:)

> 1. presented = pre + sent + ed
>
> 2. unstretchable = un + stretch + able
>
> 3. careless = care + less
>
> 4. resigning = re + sign + ing
>
> 5. unclearest = un + clear + est
>
> 6. helplessness = help + less + ness

- Check your work. Make an **X** next to any item you got wrong. ✔

Word Introduction

a. (Write on the board:)

> different
> prove
> speak
> pinch
> pure

b. Get ready to read these words.
- First word: **different.** What word? (Signal.) *Different.*
c. Next word: **prove.** What word? (Signal.) *Prove.*
- (Repeat for: **speak, pinch, pure.**)
d. Now spell those words.
- Spell **different.** Get ready. (Signal.) *D-I-F-F-E-R-E-N-T.*
e. Spell **prove.** Get ready. (Signal.) *P-R-O-V-E.*
- (Repeat for: **speak, pinch, pure.**)
f. (Erase the board.)
- Spell the words without looking.
g. Spell **different.** Get ready. (Signal.) *D-I-F-F-E-R-E-N-T.*
h. Spell **prove.** Get ready. (Signal.) *P-R-O-V-E.*
- (Repeat for: **speak, pinch, pure.**)

Word Building

a. You're going to write some words made up of more than one morphograph.
- Number your paper from 1 to 6. ✔
b. Word 1: **helpless.**
- What's the first morphograph in **helpless?** (Signal.) *Help.*
- Next morphograph? (Signal.) *Less.*
c. Write **helpless.** ✔
d. Word 2: **misspelled.**
- What's the first morphograph in **misspelled?** (Signal.) *Mis.*
- Next morphograph? (Signal.) *Spell.*
- Next morphograph? (Signal.) *E-D.*
e. Write **misspelled.** ✔
f. (Repeat steps d–e for: **3. dark, er; 4. pre, view, ed; 5. un, even; 6. port, able.**)

g. Check your work. Make an **X** next to any word you got wrong.
h. Word 1. Spell **helpless.** Get ready. (Tap for each letter.) *H-E-L-P-L-E-S-S.*
- (Repeat for: **2. misspelled, 3. darker, 4. previewed, 5. uneven, 6. portable.**)

Spelling Review

a. You're going to spell words.
b. Word 1 is **darkly.** Spell **darkly.** Get ready. (Signal.) *D-A-R-K-L-Y.*
c. Word 2 is **sketch.** Spell **sketch.** Get ready. (Signal.) *S-K-E-T-C-H.*
d. Word 3 is **thoughtful.** Spell **thoughtful.** Get ready. (Signal.) *T-H-O-U-G-H-T-F-U-L.*
e. Word 4 is **style.** Spell **style.** Get ready. (Signal.) *S-T-Y-L-E.*
f. Word 5 is **school.** Spell **school.** Get ready. (Signal.) *S-C-H-O-O-L.*
g. Word 6 is **quiet.** Spell **quiet.** Get ready. (Signal.) *Q-U-I-E-T.*
h. Word 7 is **charging.** Spell **charging.** Get ready. (Signal.) *C-H-A-R-G-I-N-G.*
i. Word 8 is **hopeless.** Spell **hopeless.** Get ready. (Signal.) *H-O-P-E-L-E-S-S.*
j. (Give individual turns on: **1. darkly, 2. sketch, 3. thoughtful, 4. style, 5. school, 6. quiet, 7. charging, 8. hopeless.**)

LESSON 15

EXERCISE 1

Affix Introduction

a. (Write on the board:)

> 1. hope + ful =
> 2. wrong + ful =
> 3. care + ful =

- All these words have the morphograph **ful.**
b. Copy the morphographs from the board on lined paper. ✔
c. Add the morphographs together to make new words. ✔
d. Check your work. Make an **X** next to any word you got wrong.
e. Word 1. Spell **hopeful.** Get ready. (Tap for each letter.) *H-O-P-E-F-U-L.*
- (Repeat for: **2. wrongful, 3. careful.**)

EXERCISE 2

Morphographic Analysis

a. (Write on the board:)

> 1. helplessly = _____
>
> 2. misspending = _____
>
> 3. equally = _____
>
> 4. frightful = _____
>
> 5. previewed= _____
>
> 6. hopelessness = _____

- Number your paper from 1 to 6. ✔
- Write the morphographs that go in each blank. Put plus signs between the morphographs. ✔

b. (Write to show:)

> 1. helplessly = help + less + ly
>
> 2. misspending = mis + spend + ing
>
> 3. equally = equal + ly
>
> 4. frightful = fright + ful
>
> 5. previewed = pre + view + ed
>
> 6. hopelessness = hope + less + ness

c. Check your work. Make an **X** next to any item you got wrong. ✔

EXERCISE 3

Prompted Review

a. (Write on the board:)

> 1. speak
> 2. wreck
> 3. sketch
> 4. thought
> 5. different
> 6. person
> 7. choice
> 8. prove

b. Word 1 is **speak.** Spell **speak.** Get ready. (Signal.) *S-P-E-A-K.*
c. Word 2 is **wreck.** Spell **wreck.** Get ready. (Signal.) *W-R-E-C-K.*
d. (Repeat step c for: **3. sketch, 4. thought, 5. different, 6. person, 7. choice, 8. prove.**)
e. (Erase the board.)
- Now spell those words without looking.
f. Word 1 is **speak.** Spell **speak.** Get ready. (Signal.) *S-P-E-A-K.*
g. Word 2 is **wreck.** Spell **wreck.** Get ready. (Signal.) *W-R-E-C-K.*
h. (Repeat step g for: **3. sketch, 4. thought, 5. different, 6. person, 7. choice, 8. prove.**)
i. (Give individual turns on **1. speak, 2. wreck, 3. sketch, 4. thought, 5. different, 6. person, 7. choice, 8. prove.**)

Affix Introduction

a. (Write on the board:)

> 1. pack + age =
> 2. wreck + age =
> 3. use + age =

- All these words have the morphograph **a-g-e.**
b. Number your paper from 1 to 3. ✔
c. Add the morphographs together to make new words. ✔
d. Check your work. Make an **X** next to any word you got wrong.
e. Word 1. Spell **package.** Get ready. (Tap for each letter.) *P-A-C-K-A-G-E.*
- (Repeat for: **2. wreckage, 3. usage.**)

Word Building

a. (Write on the board:)

> 1. help + ful + ly = _____
> 2. care + less + ness = _____
> 3. un + prove + en = _____
> 4. re + serve = _____
> 5. quiet + est = _____
> 6. stretch + able = _____

b. You're going to write the words that go in the blanks.
- Number your paper from 1 to 6. ✔
c. Word 1. Write **helpfully** on your paper. ✔
d. Do the rest of the words on your own. ✔
e. Check your work. Make an **X** next to any word you got wrong.
f. Word 1. Spell **helpfully.** Get ready. (Tap for each letter.) *H-E-L-P-F-U-L-L-Y.*
- (Repeat for: **2. carelessness, 3. unproven, 4. reserve, 5. quietest, 6. stretchable.**)

Spelling Review

a. You're going to spell words.
b. Word 1 is **thought.** Spell **thought.** Get ready. (Signal.) *T-H-O-U-G-H-T.*
c. Word 2 is **preview.** Spell **preview.** Get ready. (Signal.) *P-R-E-V-I-E-W.*
d. Word 3 is **wreck.** Spell **wreck.** Get ready. (Signal.) *W-R-E-C-K.*
e. Word 4 is **curable.** Spell **curable.** Get ready. (Signal.) *C-U-R-A-B-L-E.*
f. Word 5 is **style.** Spell **style.** Get ready. (Signal.) *S-T-Y-L-E.*
g. Word 6 is **caught.** Spell **caught.** Get ready. (Signal.) *C-A-U-G-H-T.*
h. (Give individual turns on: **1. thought, 2. preview, 3. wreck, 4. curable, 5. style, 6. caught.**)

EXERCISE 1

Affix Introduction

a. (Write on the board:)

> 1. rent + al =
> 2. form + al =
> 3. verb + al =

- All these words have the morphograph **a-l.**
b. Number your paper from 1 to 3. ✔
c. Add the morphographs together. Write just the new words. ✔
d. Check your work. Make an **X** next to any word you got wrong.
e. Word 1. Spell **rental.** Get ready. (Tap for each letter.) *R-E-N-T-A-L.*
- (Repeat for: **2. formal, 3. verbal.**)

EXERCISE 2

Morphographic Analysis

a. (Write on the board:)

> 1. usable = _____
>
> 2. careless = _____
>
> 3. pleasing = _____
>
> 4. liked = _____
>
> 5. removable = _____
>
> 6. building = _____

- Number your paper from 1 to 6. ✔
- These words are made up of more than one morphograph. You're going to write the morphographs that go in each blank.
b. **Usable** What's the first morphograph in **usable?** (Signal.) *Use.*
c. Item 1. Write **use** and a plus sign. Don't forget to write the **e** at the end of **use.** ✔
d. What's the next morphograph in **usable?** (Signal.) *Able.*
e. Write **able.** ✔

f. Your paper should look like this:
- (Write to show:)

> 1. usable = use + able

g. Do the rest of the words on your own. You have to write an **e** at the end of some of the morphographs. ✔
- (Write to show:)

> 1. usable = use + able
>
> 2. careless = care + less
>
> 3. pleasing = please + ing
>
> 4. liked = like + ed
>
> 5. removable = re + move + able
>
> 6. building = build + ing

h. Check your work. Make an **X** next to any item you got wrong. ✔

EXERCISE 3

Spelling Review

a. You're going to spell words.
b. Word 1 is **wrecked.** Spell **wrecked.** Get ready. (Signal.) *W-R-E-C-K-E-D.*
c. Word 2 is **several.** Spell **several.** Get ready. (Signal.) *S-E-V-E-R-A-L.*
d. Word 3 is **charging.** Spell **charging.** Get ready. (Signal.) *C-H-A-R-G-I-N-G.*
e. Word 4 is **different.** Spell **different.** Get ready. (Signal.) *D-I-F-F-E-R-E-N-T.*
f. Word 5 is **thought.** Spell **thought.** Get ready. (Signal.) *T-H-O-U-G-H-T.*
g. Word 6 is **style.** Spell **style.** Get ready. (Signal.) *S-T-Y-L-E.*
h. Word 7 is **glory.** Spell **glory.** Get ready. (Signal.) *G-L-O-R-Y.*
i. Word 8 is **people.** Spell **people.** Get ready. (Signal.) *P-E-O-P-L-E.*
j. (Give individual turns on: **1. wrecked, 2. several, 3. charging, 4. different, 5. thought, 6. style, 7. glory, 8. people.**)

LESSON 18

EXERCISE 1

Affix Introduction

a. (Write on the board:)

> 1. fool + ish =
> 2. child + ish =
> 3. self + ish =

- All these words have the morphograph **ish.**
b. Number your paper from 1 to 3. ✔
c. Add the morphographs together. Write just the new words. ✔
d. Check your work. Make an **X** next to any word you got wrong.
e. Word 1. Spell **foolish.** Get ready. (Tap for each letter.) *F-O-O-L-I-S-H.*
- (Repeat for: **2. childish, 3. selfish.**)

EXERCISE 2

Word Building

a. (Write on the board:)

> 1. use + age = _____
> 2. care + less + ly = _____
> 3. thought + ful + ness = _____
> 4. wreck + age = _____
> 5. fine + al = _____
> 6. pack + age + ing = _____

b. You're going to write the words that go in the blanks.
- Number your paper from 1 to 6. ✔
c. Word 1. Write **usage** on your paper. ✔
d. Do the rest of the words on your own. ✔
e. Check your work. Make an **X** next to any word you got wrong.
f. Word 1. Spell **usage.** Get ready. (Tap for each letter.) *U-S-A-G-E.*
- (Repeat for: **2. carelessly, 3. thoughtfulness, 4. wreckage, 5. final, 6. packaging.**)

EXERCISE 3

Prompted Review

a. (Write on the board:)

> 1. speaker
> 2. purely
> 3. wrongfully
> 4. formal
> 5. grudge
> 6. straightest
> 7. signal
> 8. stretcher

b. Word 1 is **speaker.** Spell **speaker.** Get ready. (Signal.) *S-P-E-A-K-E-R.*
c. Word 2 is **purely.** Spell **purely.** Get ready. (Signal.) *P-U-R-E-L-Y.*
d. (Repeat step *c* for: **3. wrongfully, 4. formal, 5. grudge, 6. straightest, 7. signal, 8. stretcher.**)
e. (Erase the board.)
- Now spell those words without looking.
f. Word 1 is **speaker.** Spell **speaker.** Get ready. (Signal.) *S-P-E-A-K-E-R.*
g. Word 2 is **purely.** Spell **purely.** Get ready. (Signal.) *P-U-R-E-L-Y.*
h. (Repeat step *g* for: **3. wrongfully, 4. formal, 5. grudge, 6. straightest, 7. signal, 8. stretcher.**)
i. (Give individual turns on **1. speaker, 2. purely, 3. wrongfully, 4. formal, 5. grudge, 6. straightest, 7. signal, 8. stretcher.**)

EXERCISE 1

Word Introduction

> *Note:* Use context sentence for **vary***.

a. (Write on the board:)

> hurry
> study
> pity
> deny
> copy
> glory
> vary
> heavy

b. Get ready to read these words.
- First word: **hurry.** What word? (Signal.) *Hurry.*
c. Next word: **study.** What word? (Signal.) *Study.*
- (Repeat for: **pity, deny, copy, glory, vary*, heavy.**)
d. Now spell those words.
- Spell **hurry.** Get ready. (Signal.) *H-U-R-R-Y.*
e. Spell **study.** Get ready. (Signal.) *S-T-U-D-Y.*
- (Repeat for: **pity, deny, copy, glory, vary, heavy.**)
f. (Erase the board.)
- Spell the words without looking.
g. Spell **hurry.** Get ready. (Signal.) *H-U-R-R-Y.*
h. Spell **study.** Get ready. (Signal.) *S-T-U-D-Y.*
- (Repeat for: **pity, deny, copy, glory, vary, heavy.**)

EXERCISE 2

Vowels and Consonants
a. (Write on the board:)

> 1. r a n c h   3. s c r u b
>
> 2. p l a n   4. p r i n t

- Copy the words. Skip a line between each word. Raise your hand when you're finished. ✔
b. You're going to write **c** or **v** above each letter of the words. You'll write **c** above the consonants and **v** above the vowels.
- Everybody, what will you write above the consonants? (Signal.) *C.*
- What will you write above the vowels? (Signal.) *V.*
- Tell me the vowel letters. Get ready. (Signal.) *A, E, I, O, U.*
c. Word 1 is **ranch.** The first letter is **r.** Is that a vowel or a consonant? (Signal.) *Consonant.*
- The next letter is **a.** Is that a vowel or a consonant? (Signal.) *Vowel.*
- The next letter is **n.** Is that a vowel or a consonant? (Signal.) *Consonant.*
- The next letter is **c.** Is that a vowel or a consonant? (Signal.) *Consonant.*
- The last letter is **h.** Is that a vowel or a consonant? (Signal.) *Consonant.*
d. Write **c** or **v** above each letter in the word **ranch.** Raise your hand when you're finished.
(Observe students and give feedback.)
- (Write to show:)

> c v c c c
> 1. r a n c h

- Check your work. Here's what you should have. Make an **X** next to the word **ranch** if you got it wrong. ✔
e. Do the rest of the words. Write **c** or **v** above each letter. Raise your hand when you're finished.
(Observe students and give feedback.)
f. (Write to show:)

> c v c c c   c c c v c
> 1. r a n c h   3. s c r u b
> c c v c   c c v c c
> 2. p l a n   4. p r i n t

- Check your work. Here's what you should have. Make an **X** next to any word you got wrong. ✔

Prompted Review

a. (Write on the board:)

> 1. carelessly
> 2. foolishness
> 3. previewed
> 4. several
> 5. might
> 6. people
> 7. happy
> 8. movable

b. Word 1 is **carelessly.** Spell **carelessly.** Get ready. (Signal.) *C-A-R-E-L-E-S-S-L-Y.*

c. Word 2 is **foolishness.** Spell **foolishness.** Get ready. (Signal.) *F-O-O-L-I-S-H-N-E-S-S.*

d. (Repeat step *c* for: **3. previewed, 4. several, 5. might, 6. people, 7. happy, 8. movable.**)

e. (Erase the board.)

● Now spell those words without looking.

f. Word 1 is **carelessly.** Spell **carelessly.** Get ready. (Signal.) *C-A-R-E-L-E-S-S-L-Y.*

g. Word 2 is **foolishness.** Spell **foolishness.** Get ready. (Signal.) *F-O-O-L-I-S-H-N-E-S-S.*

h. (Repeat step *g* for: **3. previewed, 4. several, 5. might, 6. people, 7. happy, 8. movable.**)

i. (Give individual turns on **1. carelessly, 2. foolishness, 3. previewed, 4. several, 5. might, 6. people, 7. happy, 8. movable.**)

LESSON 20

EXERCISE 1

Test

a. Today you have a spelling test. Number your lined paper from 1 through 10. ✔

b. Word 1 is **different.** What word? (Signal.) *Different.*

• Write the word **different.** ✔

c. Word 2 is **straightness.** What word? (Signal.) *Straightness.*

• Write the word **straightness.** ✔

d. (Repeat step *c* for: **3. wrongful, 4. carefully, 5. selfish, 6. study, 7. signal, 8. stretching, 9. wreckage, 10. usage.**)

e. Pick up your red pen. ✔
Make an **X** next to any word spelled wrong.

• (Write on board:)

1. different	6. study
2. straightness	7. signal
3. wrongful	8. stretching
4. carefully	9. wreckage
5. selfish	10. usage

• Write the correct spelling next to any word you spelled wrong.
(Observe students and give feedback.)

LESSON 21

EXERCISE 1

Affix Introduction

a. (Write on the board:)

> 1. rain + y =
> 2. sleep + y =
> 3. jump + y =

- All these words have the morphograph **y.**
b. Number your paper from 1 to 3. ✔
c. Add the morphographs together. Write just the new words. ✔
d. Check your work. Make an **X** next to any word you got wrong.
e. Word 1. Spell **rainy.** Get ready. (Tap for each letter.) *R-A-I-N-Y.*
- (Repeat for: **2. sleepy, 3. jumpy.**)

EXERCISE 2

Doubling Rule

a. (Write on the board:)

> spot + ing =
>
> spot + less =

b. When we add a morphograph to a word that ends with **cvc,** we sometimes have to change the spelling of that word.
- Here is the rule: Double the final consonant when the next morphograph begins with a vowel letter.
c. My turn: When do you double the final consonant? When the next morphograph begins with a vowel letter.
- Your turn: When do you double the final consonant? (Signal.) *When the next morphograph begins with a vowel letter.*
d. That's right: When the next morphograph begins with a vowel letter.

e. (Point to **ing** on the board.)
- Does **ing** begin with a vowel letter or a consonant letter? (Signal.) *A vowel letter.*
- (Write to show:)

> v
> spot + ing =
>
> spot + less =

f. The morphograph **ing** begins with a vowel letter, so we have to double the final consonant in **spot** when we add **ing.**
- (Write to show:)

> v   ↓
> spot + ing = spotting
>
> spot + less =

g. (Point to **less** on the board.)
- Does **less** begin with a vowel letter or a consonant letter? (Signal.) *A consonant letter.*
- (Write to show:)

> v   ↓
> spot + ing = spotting
> c
> spot + less =

h. The morphograph **less** does not begin with a vowel letter, so we don't have to double the final consonant in **spot** when we add **less.**
- (Write to show:)

> v   ↓
> spot + ing = spotting
> c
> spot + less = spotless

i. Everyone, spell **spotting.** Get ready. (Tap for each letter.) *S-P-O-T-T-I-N-G.*
j. Now spell **spotless.** Get ready. (Tap for each letter.) *S-P-O-T-L-E-S-S.*

Morphographic Analysis

a. (Write on the board:)

> 1. global = _____
>
> 2. finely = _____
>
> 3. served = _____
>
> 4. usage = _____
>
> 5. thoughtful = _____
>
> 6. quieter = _____

- Number your paper from 1 to 6. ✔
- These words are made up of more than one morphograph. You're going to write the morphographs that go in each blank.

b. **Global.** What's the first morphograph in **global?** (Signal.) *Globe.*

c. Item 1. Write **globe** and a plus sign. Don't forget to write the **e** at the end of **globe.** ✔

d. What's the next morphograph in **global?** (Signal.) *Al.*

e. Write **a-l.** ✔

f. Your paper should look like this:

- (Write to show:)

> **1. global = globe + al**

g. Do the rest of the words on your own. You have to write an **e** at the end of some of the morphographs. ✔

- (Write to show:)

> **1. global = globe + al**
>
> **2. finely = fine + ly**
>
> **3. served = serve + ed**
>
> **4. usage = use + age**
>
> **5. thoughtful = thought + ful**
>
> **6. quieter = quiet + er**

h. Check your work. Make an **X** next to any item you got wrong.

LESSON 22

EXERCISE 1

Y as a Vowel Letter

a. (Write on the board:)

> y

b. **Y** is usually a consonant letter, but sometimes it's a vowel letter.
c. Here is the rule: If **y** is at the end of a morphograph, then it is a vowel letter.
- Listen again: (Repeat the rule.)
d. (Write to show:)

> y
> 1. happy
> 2. boy
> 3. you
> 4. yellow
> 5. berry
> 6. play

e. Number 1 is **happy.**
- Is the **y** a vowel letter or a consonant letter in the word **happy?** (Signal.) *A vowel letter.*
- How do you know? (Signal.) *It's at the end of a morphograph.*
f. Number 2 is **boy.**
- Is the **y** a vowel letter or a consonant letter in the word **boy?** (Signal.) *A vowel letter.*
- How do you know? (Signal.) *It's at the end of a morphograph.*
g. Number 3 is **you.**
- Is the **y** a vowel letter or a consonant letter in the word **you?** (Signal.) *A consonant letter.*
- How do you know? (Signal.) *It's not at the end of a morphograph.*
h. (Repeat step *g* for: **4. yellow.**)
i. Number 5 is **berry.**
- Is the **y** a vowel letter or a consonant letter in the word **berry?** (Signal.) *A vowel letter.*
- How do you know? (Signal.) *It's at the end of a morphograph.*
j. (Repeat step *i* for: **6. play.**)

EXERCISE 2

Doubling Rule

a. (Write on the board:)

> 1. run + ing =
> 2. drip + less =
> 3. fad + ish =
> 4. grab + ed =
> 5. fret + ful =

b. Number your paper from 1 through 5. ✔
Copy the board on your paper with the plus and equal signs. ✔
c. Remember, when we add a morphograph to a word that ends **cvc,** we sometimes have to change the spelling of that word.
- Here is the rule: Double the final consonant when the next morphograph begins with a vowel letter.
d. When do you double the final consonant? (Signal.) *When the next morphograph begins with a vowel letter.*
e. That's right: When the next morphograph begins with a vowel letter.
f. (Point to **ing** on the board:) Does this suffix begin with a vowel letter or a consonant letter? (Signal.) *A vowel letter.*
g. The morphograph **ing** begins with a vowel letter, so we have to double the final consonant in **run** when we add **ing.**
h. Write **running** after the equal sign for word 1. ✔
i. Finish the words on your own. ✔
j. Check your work. Make an **X** next to any word you got wrong.
k. Word 1. Spell **running.** Get ready. (Tap for each letter.) *R-U-N-N-I-N-G.*
- (Repeat for: **2. dripless, 3. faddish, 4. grabbed, 5. fretful.**)

EXERCISE 3

Spelling Review

a. You're going to spell words.

b. Word 1 is **thought.** Spell **thought.** Get ready. (Signal.) *T-H-O-U-G-H-T.*

c. Word 2 is **package.** Spell **package.** Get ready. (Signal.) *P-A-C-K-A-G-E.*

d. Word 3 is **misprinted.** Spell **misprinted.** Get ready. (Signal.) *M-I-S-P-R-I-N-T-E-D.*

e. Word 4 is **worldly.** Spell **worldly.** Get ready. (Signal.) *W-O-R-L-D-L-Y.*

f. Word 5 is **speak.** Spell **speak.** Get ready. (Signal.) *S-P-E-A-K.*

g. Word 6 is **sketch.** Spell **sketch.** Get ready. (Signal.) *S-K-E-T-C-H.*

h. (Give individual turns on: **1. thought, 2. package, 3. misprinted, 4. worldly, 5. speak, 6. sketch.**)

EXERCISE 1

Word Introduction

a. (Write on the board:)

> length
> strength
> skate
> study
> carry
> fancy
> value

b. Get ready to read these words.
- First word: **length.** What word? (Signal.) *Length.*
c. Next word: **strength.** What word? (Signal.) *Strength.*
- (Repeat for: **skate, study, carry, fancy, value.**)
d. Now spell those words.
- Spell **length.** Get ready. (Signal.) *L-E-N-G-T-H.*
e. Spell **strength.** Get ready. (Signal.) *S-T-R-E-N-G-T-H.*
- (Repeat for: **skate, study, carry, fancy, value.**)
f. (Erase the board.)
- Spell the words without looking.
g. Spell **length.** Get ready. (Signal.) *L-E-N-G-T-H.*
h. Spell **strength.** Get ready. (Signal.) *S-T-R-E-N-G-T-H.*
- (Repeat for: **skate, study, carry, fancy, value.**)

EXERCISE 2

Doubling Rule

a. (Write on the board:)

> 1. swim + ing =
> 2. sun + y =
> 3. spot + less =
> 4. stop + ed =
> 5. star + ing =
> 6. mad + ness =

b. Number your paper from 1 through 6. ✔
   Copy the board on your paper with the plus and equal signs. ✔

c. Remember, when we add a morphograph to a word that ends **cvc,** we sometimes have to change the spelling of that word.
- Here is the rule: Double the final consonant when the next morphograph begins with a vowel letter.
d. When do you double the final consonant? (Signal.) *When the next morphograph begins with a vowel letter.*
e. That's right: When the next morphograph begins with a vowel letter.
f. (Point to **ing** on the board.)
- Does this suffix begin with a vowel letter or a consonant letter? (Signal.) *A vowel letter.*
g. The morphograph **ing** begins with a vowel letter, so we have to double the final consonant in **swim** when we add **ing.**
h. Write **swimming** after the equals sign for word 1. ✔
i. Finish the words on your own. ✔
j. Check your work. Make an **X** next to any word you got wrong.
k. Word 1. Spell **swimming.** Get ready. (Tap for each letter.) *S-W-I-M-M-I-N-G.*
- (Repeat for: **2. sunny, 3. spotless, 4. stopped, 5. starring, 6. madness.**)

EXERCISE 3

Word Building

a. (Write on the board:)

> 1. glass + y = _____
> 2. pain + ful + ly = _____
> 3. un + end + ing = _____
> 4. thought + ful + ness = _____
> 5. un + like + able = _____
> 6. quiet + ness = _____

b. You're going to write the words that go in the blanks.
- Number your paper from 1 to 6. ✔
c. Word 1. Write **glassy** on your paper. ✔
d. Do the rest of the words on your own. ✔
e. Check your work. Make an **X** next to any word you got wrong.
f. Word 1. Spell **glassy.** Get ready. (Tap for each letter.) *G-L-A-S-S-Y.*
- (Repeat for: **2. painfully, 3. unending, 4. thoughtfulness, 5. unlikable, 6. quietness.**)

LESSON 24

EXERCISE 1

Word Introduction

> *Note:* Pronounce the sound /ō/ like the letter name **O**.

a. (Write on the board:)

> boat
> float
> goat
> throat
> groan
> goal

b. Get ready to read these words.
- In each of these words, the sound /ō/ is spelled **o-a.**
- First word: **boat.** What word? (Signal.) *Boat.*

c. Next word: **float.** What word? (Signal.) *Float.*
- (Repeat for: **goat, throat, groan, goal.**)

d. Now spell those words.
- Spell **boat.** Get ready. (Signal.) *B-O-A-T.*

e. Spell **float.** Get ready. (Signal.) *F-L-O-A-T.*
- (Repeat for: **goat, throat, groan, goal.**)

f. (Erase the board.)

- Spell the words without looking.

g. Spell **boat.** Get ready. (Signal.) *B-O-A-T.*

h. Spell **float.** Get ready. (Signal.) *F-L-O-A-T.*
- (Repeat for: **goat, throat, groan, goal.**)

EXERCISE 2

Doubling Rule

a. (Write on the board:)

> 1. hop + ing =
> 2. wish + ful =
> 3. start + ing =
> 4. trap + ed =
> 5. sad + ness =

b. Number your paper from 1 through 5. ✔ Copy the board on your paper with the plus and equal signs. ✔

c. When do you double the final consonant? (Call on a student.) *When a word ends CVC and the next morphograph begins with a vowel letter.*

- Yes: When a word ends **cvc** and the next morphograph begins with a vowel letter.

d. Everybody. When do you double the final consonant? (Signal.) *When a word ends CVC and the next morphograph begins with a vowel letter.*
- (Repeat until firm.)

e. Some of these words follow the rule about doubling the final consonant of words that end **cvc.** Do all these words on your own. ✔

f. Check your work. Make an **X** next to any word you got wrong.

g. Word 1. Spell **hopping.** Get ready. (Tap for each letter.) *H-O-P-P-I-N-G.*
- (Repeat for: **2. wishful, 3. starting, 4. trapped, 5. sadness.**)

EXERCISE 3

Prompted Review

> *Note:* Use context sentence for **vary** *.

a. (Write on the board:)

> 1. glory
> 2. vary
> 3. strength
> 4. sleepy
> 5. served
> 6. selfish

b. Word 1 is **glory.** Spell **glory.** Get ready. (Signal.) *G-L-O-R-Y.*

c. Word 2 is **vary*.** Spell **vary.** Get ready. (Signal.) *V-A-R-Y.*

d. (Repeat step c for: **3. strength, 4. sleepy, 5. served, 6. selfish.**)

d. (Erase the board.)

- Now spell those words without looking.

f. Word 1 is **glory.** Spell **glory.** Get ready. (Signal.) *G-L-O-R-Y.*

g. Word 2 is **vary.** Spell **vary.** Get ready. (Signal.) *V-A-R-Y.*

h. (Repeat step g for: **3. strength, 4. sleepy, 5. served, 6. selfish.**)

i. (Give individual turns on **1. glory, 2. vary, 3. strength, 4. sleepy, 5. served, 6. selfish.**)

EXERCISE 1

Consonant-and-Y

a. Later, you are going to learn about words that end with **consonant-and-y.**

b. (Write on the board:)

> **1. study**
> **2. play**
> **3. pity**
> **4. hurry**

c. (Point to the **d** in **study.**)

• Everybody, is this a vowel letter or a consonant letter? (Signal.) *A consonant letter.*

d. **D** is a consonant letter, so **study** ends **consonant-and-y.**

e. (Point to the **a** in **play.**)

• Everybody, is this a vowel letter or a consonant letter? (Signal.) *A vowel letter.*

f. **A** is a vowel letter, so **play** does not end **consonant-and-y.**

g. (Point to the **t** in **pity.**)

• Everybody, is this a vowel letter or a consonant letter? (Signal.) *A consonant letter.*

h. **T** is a consonant letter, so **pity** ends **consonant-and-y.**

i. (Point to the second **r** in **hurry.**)

• Everybody, is this a vowel letter or a consonant letter? (Signal.) *A consonant letter.*

j. **R** is a consonant letter, so **hurry** ends **consonant-and-y.**

EXERCISE 2

Morphographic Analysis

a. (Write on the board:)

> **1. winner =** _____
>
> **2. sadness =** _____
>
> **3. saddest =** _____
>
> **4. cutting =** _____
>
> **5. fitness =** _____
>
> **6. hopping =** _____

• Number your paper from 1 to 6. ✔

b. These words are made up of more than one morphograph. You're going to write the morphographs that go in each blank.

c. **Winner.** What's the first morphograph in **winner?** (Signal.) *Win.*

d. Item 1. Write **win** and a plus sign. Don't forget to write **win** with just one **n.** ✔

e. What's the next morphograph in **winner?** (Signal.) *Er.*

f. Write **e-r.** ✔

g. Your paper should look like this:

• (Write to show:)

> **1. winner = win + er**

h. Do the rest of the words on your own. You have to "undouble" the final consonant of some of the morphographs. ✔

i. (Write to show:)

1. winner = win + er

2. sadness = sad + ness

3. saddest = sad + est

4. cutting = cut + ing

5. fitness = fit + ness

6. hopping = hop + ing

j. Check your work. Make an **X** next to any item you got wrong. ✔

Spelling Review

a. Get ready to spell and write some words.

b. Word 1 is **strength.**
- What word? (Signal.) *Strength.*
- Spell **strength.** Get ready. (Signal.) *S-T-R-E-N-G-T-H.*
- Write it. ✔

c. Word 2 is **sleepy.**
- What word? (Signal.) *Sleepy.*
- Spell **sleepy.** Get ready. (Signal.) *S-L-E-E-P-Y.*
- Write it. ✔

d. (Repeat step c for: **3. fancy, 4. groan, 5. heavy.**)

e. I'll spell each word.
- Put an **X** next to any word you missed and write that word correctly.
- (Spell each word twice. Write the words on the board as you spell them.)

1. strength   4. groan

2. sleepy   5. heavy

3. fancy

EXERCISE 1

Consonant-and-Y

a.   Later, you are going to learn about words that end with **consonant-and-y.**

b.   (Write on the board:)

> **1. rusty**
> **2. deny**
> **3. money**
> **4. stormy**

c.   (Point to the **t** in **rusty.**)

•   Everybody, is this a vowel letter or a consonant letter? (Signal.) *A consonant letter.*

d.   **T** is a consonant letter, so **rusty** ends **consonant-and-y.**

e.   (Point to the **n** in **deny.**)

•   Everybody, is this a vowel letter or a consonant letter? (Signal.) *A consonant letter.*

f.   **N** is a consonant letter, so **deny** ends **consonant-and-y.**

g.   (Point to the **e** in **money.**)

•   Everybody, is this a vowel letter or a consonant letter? (Signal.) *A vowel letter.*

h.   **E** is a vowel letter, so **money** ends **vowel-and-y.**

i.   (Point to the **m** in **stormy.**)

•   Everybody, is this a vowel letter or a consonant letter? (Signal.) *A consonant letter.*

j.   **M** is a consonant letter, so **stormy** ends **consonant-and-y.**

EXERCISE 2

Doubling Rule

a.   (Write on the board:)

> **1. mad + ness =**
> **2. spin + er =**
> **3. rob + ing =**
> **4. pup + y =**
> **5. leg + less =**

b.   Number your paper from 1 through 5. ✔ Copy the board on your paper with the plus and equal signs. ✔

c.   When do you double the final consonant? (Call on a student.) *When a word ends CVC and the next morphograph begins with a vowel letter.*

•   Yes: When a word ends **cvc** and the next morphograph begins with a vowel letter.

d.   Everybody, when do you double the final consonant? (Signal.) *When a word ends CVC and the next morphograph begins with a vowel letter.*

•   (Repeat until firm.)

e.   Some of these words follow the rule about doubling the final consonant of words that end **cvc.** Do all these words on your own. ✔

f.   Check your work. Make an **X** next to any word you got wrong.

g.   Word 1. Spell **madness.** Get ready. (Tap for each letter.) *M-A-D-N-E-S-S.*

•   (Repeat for: **2. spinner, 3. robbing, 4. puppy, 5. legless.**)

EXERCISE 3

Prompted Review

a.   (Write on the board:)

> **1. throat**
> **2. strength**
> **3. heavy**
> **4. prove**
> **5. style**
> **6. unclear**

b.   Word 1 is **throat.** Spell **throat.** Get ready. (Signal.) *T-H-R-O-A-T.*

c.   Word 2 is **strength.** Spell **strength.** Get ready. (Signal.) *S-T-R-E-N-G-T-H.*

d.   (Repeat step c for: **3. heavy, 4. prove, 5. style, 6. unclear.**)

e.   (Erase the board.)

•   Now spell those words without looking.

f.   Word 1 is **throat.** Spell **throat.** Get ready. (Signal.) *T-H-R-O-A-T.*

g.   Word 2 is **strength.** Spell **strength.** Get ready. (Signal.) *S-T-R-E-N-G-T-H.*

h.   (Repeat step g for: **3. heavy, 4. prove, 5. style, 6. unclear.**)

i.   (Give individual turns on **1. throat, 2. strength, 3. heavy, 4. prove, 5. style, 6. unclear.**)

EXERCISE 1

S and ES

a. (Write on board:)

s	z	sh	ch

- If words end in any of these letters or letter combinations, you add **e-s** instead of **s.**
b. Listen: **catch.** What letters does it end in? (Signal.) *C-H.*
- So do you add **s** or **e-s?** (Signal.) *E-S.*
- Yes, the word is **catches.** You can hear the **e-s.**
c. Listen: **buzz.** What letter does it end in? (Signal.) *Z.*
- So do you add **s** or **e-s?** (Signal.) *E-S.*
- Yes, the word is **buzzes.** You can hear the **e-s.**
d. Listen: **hat.** What letter does it end in? (Signal.) *T.*
- So do you add **s** or **e-s?** (Signal.) *S.*
- Yes, the word is **hats.** There is no **e-s** sound at the end.
e. Listen: **dress.** What letter does it end in? (Signal.) *S.*
- So do you add **s** or **e-s?** (Signal.) *E-S.*
- Yes, the word is **dresses.** You can hear the **e-s.**
f. Listen: **star.** What letter does it end in? (Signal.) *R.*
- So do you add **s** or **e-s?** (Signal.) *S.*
- Yes, the word is **stars.** There is no **e-s** sound at the end.
g. Listen: **push.** What letters does it end in? (Signal.) *S-H.*
- So do you add **s** or **e-s?** (Signal.) *E-S.*
- Yes, the word is **pushes.** You can hear the **e-s.**

EXERCISE 2

Affix Introduction

a. (Write on the board:)

> 1. **loose + en =**
> 2. **tough + en =**
> 3. **fall + en =**

- All these words have the morphograph **e-n.**
b. Number your paper from 1 to 3. ✔
c. Add the morphographs together. Write just the new words. ✔
d. Check your work. Make an **X** next to any word you got wrong.
e. Word 1. Spell **loosen.** Get ready. (Tap for each letter.) *L-O-O-S-E-N.*
- (Repeat for: **2. toughen, 3. fallen.**)

EXERCISE 3

Spelling Review

a. Get ready to spell and write some words.
b. Word 1 is **rusty.**
- What word? (Signal.) *Rusty.*
- Spell **rusty.** Get ready. (Signal.) *R-U-S-T-Y.*
- Write it. ✔
c. Word 2 is **busy.**
- What word? (Signal.) *Busy.*
- Spell **busy.** Get ready. (Signal.) *B-U-S-Y.*
- Write it. ✔
d. (Repeat step *c* for: **3. twice, 4. school, 5. quiet, 6. light.**)
e. I'll spell each word.
- Put an **X** next to any word you missed and write that word correctly.
- (Spell each word twice. Write the words on the board as you spell them.)

1. rusty	4. school
2. busy	5. quiet
3. twice	6. light

EXERCISE 1

S and ES

a. I will say some words. Tell me if each word ends in the morphograph **s** or the morphograph **e-s.**

b. Listen: **crashes.**

- What morphograph does it end in? (Signal.) *E-S.*

c. Listen: **lights.**

- What morphograph does it end in? (Signal.) *S.*

d. Listen: **shops.** What morphograph does it end in? (Signal.) *S.*

e. (Repeat step *d* for: **washes, deals, presses, bars, forms.**)

f. Let's spell some of those words.

g. First word: **lights.** What word? (Signal.) *Lights.*

- Spell **lights.** Get ready. (Tap for each letter.) *L-I-G-H-T-S.*

h. (Repeat step *g* for: **presses, deals, washes.**)

EXERCISE 2

Word Building

a. (Write on the board:)

> 1. un + prove + en = _____
> 2. rock + y = _____
> 3. scare + y = _____
> 4. re + think + ing = _____
> 5. pre + school = _____
> 6. large + ness = _____

b. You're going to write the words that go in the blanks.

- Number your paper from 1 to 6. ✔

c. Word 1. Write **unproven** on your paper. ✔

d. Do the rest of the words on your own. ✔

e. Check your work. Make an **X** next to any word you got wrong.

f. Word 1. Spell **unproven.** Get ready. (Tap for each letter.) *U-N-P-R-O-V-E-N.*

- (Repeat for: **2. rocky, 3. scary, 4. rethinking, 5. preschool, 6. largeness.**)

EXERCISE 3

Prompted Review

a. (Write on the board:)

> 1. float
> 2. strength
> 3. sturdy
> 4. speak
> 5. sketch
> 6. story
> 7. together
> 8. people

b. Word 1 is **float.** Spell **float.** Get ready. (Signal.) *F-L-O-A-T.*

c. Word 2 is **strength.** Spell **strength.** Get ready. (Signal.) *S-T-R-E-N-G-T-H.*

d. (Repeat step *c* for: **3. sturdy, 4. speak, 5. sketch, 6. story, 7. together, 8. people.**)

e. (Erase the board.)

- Now spell those words without looking.

f. Word 1 is **float.** Spell **float.** Get ready. (Signal.) *F-L-O-A-T.*

g. Word 2 is **strength.** Spell **strength.** Get ready. (Signal.) *S-T-R-E-N-G-T-H.*

h. (Repeat step *g* for: **3. sturdy, 4. speak, 5. sketch, 6. story, 7. together, 8. people.**)

i. (Give individual turns on **1. float, 2. strength, 3. sturdy, 4. speak, 5. sketch, 6. story, 7. together, 8. people.**)

EXERCISE 1

Affix Introduction

a. (Write on the board:)

> 1. in + land =
> 2. in + form =
> 3. in + side =

- All these words have the morphograph **i-n.**
b. Number your paper from 1 to 3. ✔
c. Add the morphographs together. Write just the new words. ✔
d. Check your work. Make an **X** next to any word you got wrong.
e. Word 1. Spell **inland.** Get ready. (Tap for each letter.) *I-N-L-A-N-D.*
- (Repeat for: **2. inform, 3. inside.**)

EXERCISE 2

Word Building

a. (Write on the board:)

> 1. gape + ing =
> 2. win + ing =
> 3. strength + en =
> 4. stretch + er + s =
> 5. slap + ed =

b. You're going to write the words that go after the equal signs.
- Some of these words follow the final **e** rule. Some follow the doubling rule. Be careful.
- Number your paper from 1 to 5. ✔
c. Word 1. Write **gaping** on your paper. ✔
d. Do the rest of the words on your own. ✔
e. Check your work. Make an **X** next to any word you got wrong.
f. Word 1. Spell **gaping.** Get ready. (Tap for each letter.) *G-A-P-I-N-G.*
- (Repeat for: **2. winning, 3. strengthen, 4. stretchers, 5. slapped.**)

EXERCISE 3

Spelling Review

a. You're going to spell words.
b. Word 1 is **passes.** Spell **passes.** Get ready. (Signal.) *P-A-S-S-E-S.*
c. Word 2 is **preview.** Spell **preview.** Get ready. (Signal.) *P-R-E-V-I-E-W.*
d. Word 3 is **together.** Spell **together.** Get ready. (Signal.) *T-O-G-E-T-H-E-R.*
e. Word 4 is **jumpy.** Spell **jumpy.** Get ready. (Signal.) *J-U-M-P-Y.*
f. Word 5 is **goats.** Spell **goats.** Get ready. (Signal.) *G-O-A-T-S.*
g. Word 6 is **churches.** Spell **churches.** Get ready. (Signal.) *C-H-U-R-C-H-E-S.*
h. Word 7 is **another.** Spell **another.** Get ready. (Signal.) *A-N-O-T-H-E-R.*
i. Word 8 is **straightest.** Spell **straightest.** Get ready. (Signal.) *S-T-R-A-I-G-H-T-E-S-T.*
j. (Give individual turns on: **1. passes, 2. preview, 3. together, 4. jumpy, 5. goats, 6. churches, 7. another, 8. straightest.**)

LESSON 30

EXERCISE 1

Test

a. Today you have a spelling test. Number your lined paper from 1 through 10. ✔

b. Word 1 is **sleepy.** What word? (Signal.) *Sleepy.*

- Write the word **sleepy.** ✔

c. Word 2 is **spinner.** What word? (Signal.) *Spinner.*

- Write the word **spinner.** ✔

d. (Repeat step *c* for: **3. sharpen, 4. prescribe, 5. goodness, 6. stormy, 7. returned, 8. fetches, 9. resign, 10. carry.**)

e. Pick up your red pen. ✔
Make an **X** next to any word you spelled wrong.

- (Write on board:)

1. sleepy	**6. stormy**
2. spinner	**7. returned**
3. sharpen	**8. fetches**
4. prescribe	**9. resign**
5. goodness	**10. carry**

- Write the correct spelling next to any word you spelled wrong.
(Observe students and give feedback.)

EXERCISE 1

Affix Introduction

a. (Write on the board:)

> 1. con + front =
> 2. con + test =
> 3. con + strict =

- All these words have the morphograph **con.**
b. Number your paper from 1 to 3. ✔
c. Add the morphographs together. Write just the new words. ✔
d. Check your work. Make an **X** next to any word you got wrong.
e. Word 1. Spell **confront.** Get ready. (Tap for each letter.) *C-O-N-F-R-O-N-T.*
- (Repeat for: **2. contest, 3. constrict.**)

EXERCISE 2

Word Building

a. (Write on the board:)

> 1. win + er + s =
> 2. star + ed =
> 3. fine + al + ly =
> 4. noise + less + ly =
> 5. sad + ness =
> 6. breathe + ing =

b. You're going to write the words that go after the equal signs.
- Some of these words follow the final **e** rule. Some follow the doubling rule. Be careful.
- Number your paper from 1 to 6. ✔
c. Word 1: Write **winners** on your paper. ✔
d. Do the rest of the words on your own. ✔
e. Check your work. Make an **X** next to any word you got wrong.
f. Word 1. Spell **winners.** Get ready. (Tap for each letter.) *W-I-N-N-E-R-S.*
- (Repeat for: **2. starred, 3. finally, 4. noiselessly, 5. sadness, 6. breathing.**)

EXERCISE 3

Spelling Review

a. You're going to spell words.
b. Word 1 is **previewed.** Spell **previewed.** Get ready. (Signal.) *P-R-E-V-I-E-W-E-D.*
c. Word 2 is **rebuilding.** Spell **rebuilding.** Get ready. (Signal.) *R-E-B-U-I-L-D-I-N-G.*
d. Word 3 is **speaker.** Spell **speaker.** Get ready. (Signal.) *S-P-E-A-K-E-R.*
e. Word 4 is **thoughtless.** Spell **thoughtless.** Get ready. (Signal.) *T-H-O-U-G-H-T-L-E-S-S.*
f. Word 5 is **listening.** Spell **listening.** Get ready. (Signal.) *L-I-S-T-E-N-I-N-G.*
g. Word 6 is **movable.** Spell **movable.** Get ready. (Signal.) *M-O-V-A-B-L-E.*
h. (Give individual turns on: **1. previewed, 2. rebuilding, 3. speaker, 4. thoughtless, 5. listening, 6. movable.**)

LESSON 32

EXERCISE 1

S and ES

> *Note:* Pronounce the sound for **x** in step d as /**ks**/, like the ending sound in so**cks**.

a. You add **e-s** to words that end with **s, z, s-h,** and **c-h.**

b. (Write on the board:)

> **box**

c. (Point to the **x.**) We also add **e-s** to words that end with the letter **x.**

d. We don't double the **x.** Here is why: The letter **x** acts like two consonant letters because it has two consonant sounds.

• Listen: /**ks**/.

• (Repeat the sound twice more.)

e. How many consonant letters does **x** act like? (Signal.) *Two.*

f. Spell the word **boxes.** (Pause.) Get ready. (Signal.) *B-O-X-E-S.*

g. Spell the word **boxing.** (Pause.) Get ready. (Signal.) *B-O-X-I-N-G.*

h. Spell the word **taxes.** (Pause.) Get ready. (Signal.) *T-A-X-E-S.*

i. Remember, we never double an **x** when we add a morphograph.

EXERCISE 2

Morphographic Analysis

a. (Write on the board:)

> **1. winning** = _____
>
> **2. likable** = _____
>
> **3. sadness** = _____
>
> **4. final** = _____
>
> **5. snapping** = _____
>
> **6. hopeful** = _____

• Number your paper from 1 to 6. ✔

b. You're going to write the morphographs that go in each blank.

• Remember, write the morphographs the way they're spelled. You might have to add an **e** to a word or "undouble" a word.

c. Item 1. Write **win** and a plus sign. ✔

• Write the next morphograph for item 1. Do the rest of the words on your own. ✔

d. (Write to show:)

> **1. winning** = win + ing
>
> **2. likable** = like + able
>
> **3. sadness** = sad + ness
>
> **4. final** = fina + al
>
> **5. snapping** = snap + ing
>
> **6. hopeful** = hope + ful

• Check your work. Make an **X** next to any item you got wrong. ✔

Prompted Review

a. (Write on the board:)

> 1. constricted
> 2. informal
> 3. strengthen
> 4. sunny
> 5. deny
> 6. wrecking

b. Word 1 is **constricted.** Spell **constricted.** Get ready. (Signal.) *C-O-N-S-T-R-I-C-T-E-D.*

c. Word 2 is **informal.** Spell **informal.** Get ready. (Signal.) *I-N-F-O-R-M-A-L.*

d. (Repeat step *c* for: **3. strengthen, 4. sunny, 5. deny, 6. wrecking.**)

e. (Erase the board.)
- Now spell those words without looking.

f. Word 1 is **constricted.** Spell **constricted.** Get ready. (Signal.) *C-O-N-S-T-R-I-C-T-E-D.*

g. Word 2 is **informal.** Spell **informal.** Get ready. (Signal.) *I-N-F-O-R-M-A-L.*

h. (Repeat step *g* for: **3. strengthen, 4. sunny, 5. deny, 6. wrecking.**)

i. (Give individual turns on **1. constricted, 2. informal, 3. strengthen, 4. sunny, 5. deny, 6. wrecking.**)

EXERCISE 1

Consonant-and-Y

a. Later, you are going to learn about words that end with **consonant-and-y.**

b. (Write on the board:)

> **1. try**
> **2. worry**
> **3. heavy**
> **4. stay**
> **5. lonely**

c. (Point to the **r** in **try.**)
- Everybody, is this a vowel letter or a consonant letter? (Signal.) *A consonant letter.*

d. **R** is a consonant letter, so **try** ends **consonant-and-y.**

e. (Point to the second **r** in **worry.**)
- Everybody, is this a vowel letter or a consonant letter? (Signal.) *A consonant letter.*

f. **R** is a consonant letter, so **worry** ends **consonant-and-y.**

g. (Point to the **v** in **heavy.**)
- Everybody, is this a vowel letter or a consonant letter? (Signal.) *A consonant letter.*

h. **V** is a consonant letter, so **heavy** ends **consonant-and-y.**

i. (Point to the **a** in **stay.**)
- Everybody, is this a vowel letter or a consonant letter? (Signal.) *A vowel letter.*

j. **A** is a vowel letter, so **stay** does not end **consonant-and-y.**

k. (Point to the second **l** in **lonely.**)
- Everybody, is this a vowel letter or a consonant letter? (Signal.) *A consonant letter.*

l. **L** is a consonant letter, so **lonely** ends **consonant-and-y.**

EXERCISE 2

Word Introduction

> *Note:* Use context sentence for **main***.

a. (Write on the board:)

> **leave**
> **neat**
> **long**
> **main**
> **claim**
> **children**

b. Get ready to read these words.
- First word: **leave.** What word? (Signal.) *Leave.*

c. Next word: **neat.** What word? (Signal.) *Neat.*
- (Repeat for: **long, main*, claim, children.**)

d. Now spell those words.
- Spell **leave.** Get ready. (Signal.) *L-E-A-V-E.*

e. Spell **neat.** Get ready. (Signal.) *N-E-A-T.*
- (Repeat for: **long, main, claim, children.**)

f. (Erase the board.)
- Spell the words without looking.

g. Spell **leave.** Get ready. (Signal.) *L-E-A-V-E.*

h. Spell **neat.** Get ready. (Signal.) *N-E-A-T.*
- (Repeat for: **long, main, claim, children.**)

i. Get ready to write those words.

j. Word 1: **neat.** Write it. ✔
- (Repeat for: **2. leave, 3. main, 4. long, 5. children, 6. claim.**)

Spelling Review

a. You're going to spell words.

b. Word 1 is **boxing.** Spell **boxing.** Get ready. (Signal.) *B-O-X-I-N-G.*

c. Word 2 is **unproven.** Spell **unproven.** Get ready. (Signal.) *U-N-P-R-O-V-E-N.*

d. Word 3 is **constricting.** Spell **constricting.** Get ready. (Signal.) *C-O-N-S-T-R-I-C-T-I-N-G.*

e. Word 4 is **stylish.** Spell **stylish.** Get ready. (Signal.) *S-T-Y-L-I-S-H.*

f. Word 5 is **starry.** Spell **starry.** Get ready. (Signal.) *S-T-A-R-R-Y.*

g. (Give individual turns on: **1. boxing, 2. unproven, 3. constricting, 4. stylish, 5. starry.**)

Word Building

a. (Write on the board:)

> 1. in + form + al =
> 2. strength + en =
> 3. cloud + y =
> 4. fool + ish + ly =
> 5. re + start + ed =
> 6. con + fuse + ing =

b. You're going to write the words that go after the equal signs.
-   Some of these words follow the final **e** rule. Be careful.
-   Number your paper from 1 to 6. ✔
c. Word 1: Write **informal** on your paper. ✔
d. Do the rest of the words on your own. ✔
e. Check your work. Make an **X** next to any word you got wrong.
f. Word 1. Spell **informal**. Get ready. (Tap for each letter.) *I-N-F-O-R-M-A-L.*
-   (Repeat for: **2. strengthen, 3. cloudy, 4. foolishly, 5. restarted, 6. confusing.**)

Consonant-and-Y Rule

a. (Write on the board:)

> fancy + ful =
>
> fancy + er =
>
> fancy + ing =

b. When we add a morphograph to a word that ends with **consonant-and-y,** we sometimes have to change the spelling of that word.
c. Here is the rule: Change the **y** to **i** when you add a morphograph beginning with *anything*, except **i.**
-   My turn: When do you change the **y** to **i?** When the next morphograph begins with anything, except **i.**

d. Your turn: When do you change the **y** to **i?** (Signal.) *When the next morphograph begins with anything, except i.*
-   That's right: when the next morphograph begins with anything, except **i.**
e. (Point to **fancy + ful** on the board.)
-   Does **fancy** end with **consonant-and-y?** (Signal.) *Yes.*
-   The morphograph **ful** does not begin with **i,** so you have to change the **y** to **i.**
-   (Write to show:)

> **fancy + ful = fanciful**

f. (Point to **fancy + er** on the board.)
-   Does **fancy** end with **consonant-and-y?** (Signal.) *Yes.*
-   The morphograph **e-r** does not begin with **i,** so you have to change the **y** to **i.**
-   (Write to show:)

> **fancy + ful = fanciful**
>
> **fancy + er = fancier**
>
> **fancy + ing =**

g. (Point to **fancy + ing** on the board.)
-   Does **fancy** end with **consonant-and-y?** (Signal.) *Yes.*
-   The morphograph **ing** *does* begin with **i,** so you don't change the **y** to **i.**
-   (Write to show:)

> **fancy + ful = fanciful**
>
> **fancy + er = fancier**
>
> **fancy + ing = fancying**

h. Everybody, spell **fanciful.** Get ready. (Tap for each letter.) *F-A-N-C-I-F-U-L.*
-   Spell **fancier.** Get ready. (Tap for each letter.) *F-A-N-C-I-E-R.*
-   Spell **fancying.** Get ready. (Tap for each letter.) *F-A-N-C-Y-I-N-G.*

Spelling Review

a. I'm going to spell either **study, spinning,** or **stayed.**

b. Listen: **s-p-i-n-n-i-n-g.** What word? (Signal.) *Spinning.*

c. Listen: **s-t-a-y-e-d.** What word? (Signal.) *Stayed.*

d. Listen: **s-t-u-d-y.** What word? (Signal.) *Study.*

e. Get ready to spell those words.

f. Word 1. Spell **study.** Get ready. (Signal.) *S-T-U-D-Y.*

g. Word 2. Spell **spinning.** Get ready. (Signal.) *S-P-I-N-N-I-N-G.*

• (Repeat step g for **3. stayed.**)

Word Building

a. (Write on the board:)

> 1. pre + scribe + ed =
> 2. star + less =
> 3. sketch + y =
> 4. light + ness =
> 5. un + friend + ly =
> 6. re + turn + able =
> 7. star + ing =

b. You're going to write the words that go after the equal signs.
- Some of these words follow the final **e** rule. Some follow the doubling rule. Be careful.
- Number your paper from 1 to 7. ✔
c. Word 1: Write **prescribed** on your paper. ✔
d. Do the rest of the words on your own. ✔
e. Check your work. Make an **X** next to any word you got wrong.
f. Word 1. Spell **prescribed.** Get ready. (Tap for each letter.) *P-R-E-S-C-R-I-B-E-D.*
- (Repeat step *f* for: **2. starless, 3. sketchy, 4. lightness, 5. unfriendly, 6. returnable, 7. starring.**)

Consonant-and-Y Rule

a. (Write on the board:)

> pity + ed =
>
> pity + ing =
>
> pity + ful =

b. When we add a morphograph to a word that ends with **consonant-and-y,** we sometimes have to change the spelling of that word.
c. Here is the rule: Change the **y** to **i** when you add a morphograph beginning with *anything*, except **i.**
- My turn: When do you change the **y** to **i?** When the next morphograph begins with anything, except **i.**

d. Your turn: When do you change the **y** to **i?** (Signal.) *When the next morphograph begins with anything, except i.*
- That's right: when the next morphograph begins with anything, except **i.**
e. (Point to **pity + ed** on the board.)
- Does **pity** end with **consonant-and-y?** (Signal.) *Yes.*
- The morphograph **e-d** does not begin with **i,** so you have to change the **y** to **i.**
- (Write to show:)

> pity + ed = pitied

f. (Point to **pity + ing** on the board.)
- Does **pity** end with **consonant-and-y?** (Signal.) *Yes.*
- The morphograph **ing** *does* begin with **i,** so you don't change the **y** to **i.**
- (Write to show:)

> pity + ed = pitied
>
> pity + ing = pitying
>
> pity + ful =

g. (Point to **pity + ful** on the board.)
- Does **pity** end with **consonant-and-y?** (Signal.) *Yes.*
- The morphograph **ful** does not begin with **i,** so you have to change the **y** to **i.**
- (Write to show:)

> pity + ed = pitied
>
> pity + ing = pitying
>
> pity + ful = pitiful

h. Everybody, spell **pitied.** Get ready. (Tap for each letter.) *P-I-T-I-E-D.*
- Spell **pitying.** Get ready. (Tap for each letter.) *P-I-T-Y-I-N-G.*
- Spell **pitiful.** Get ready. (Tap for each letter.) *P-I-T-I-F-U-L.*

Spelling Review

a. I'm going to spell either **sunny, sadness, starring,** or **school.**

b. Listen: **s-a-d-n-e-s-s.**
What word? (Signal.) *Sadness.*

c. Listen: **s-t-a-r-r-i-n-g.**
What word? (Signal.) *Starring.*

d. Listen: **s-u-n-n-y.**
What word? (Signal.) *Sunny.*

e. Listen: **s-c-h-o-o-l.**
What word? (Signal.) *School.*

f. Get ready to spell those words.

g. Word 1. Spell **sadness.** Get ready. (Signal.)
S-A-D-N-E-S-S.

h. Word 2. Spell **starring.** Get ready. (Signal.)
S-T-A-R-R-I-N-G.

i. (Repeat for: **3. sunny, 4. school.**)

EXERCISE 1

Morphographic Analysis

a. (Write on the board:)

> 1. coming = _____
>
> 2. dragging = _____
>
> 3. furless = _____
>
> 4. final = _____
>
> 5. driving = _____
>
> 6. hopeful = _____

- Number your paper from 1 to 6. ✔
b. You're going to write the morphographs that go in each blank.
- Remember, write the morphographs the way they're spelled. You might have to add an **e** to a word or "undouble" a word. ✔
c. Item 1. Write **come** and a plus sign. ✔
d. Write the next morphograph for item 1. Do the rest of the words on your own. ✔
e. (Write to show:)

> 1. coming = come + ing
>
> 2. dragging = drag + ing
>
> 3. furless = fur + less
>
> 4. final = fine + al
>
> 5. driving = drive + ing
>
> 6. hopeful = hope +ful

- Check your work. Make an **X** next to any item you got wrong. ✔

EXERCISE 2

Consonant-and-Y Rule

a. (Write on the board:)

> 1. heavy + est =
>
> 2. lonely + ness =
>
> 3. carry + ing =
>
> 4. copy + es =
>
> 5. deny + al =
>
> 6. fancy + ful =

b. Number your paper from 1 through 6. ✔
- Each of these words ends **consonant-and-y.**
- Copy the board on your paper with the plus and equal signs. ✔
c. Remember, when we add a morphograph to a word that ends **consonant-and-y,** we usually have to change the spelling of that word.
- Here is the rule: Change the **y** to **i** when the next morphograph begins with anything, except **i.**
d. (Point to **est** on the board.)
- Does this suffix begin with an **i?** (Signal.) *No.*
e. The morphograph **est** does not begin with **i,** so we have to change the **y** to **i.**
f. Write **heaviest** after the equal sign for word 1. ✔
g. Finish the words on your own. ✔
h. Check your work. Make an **X** next to any word you got wrong.
i. Word 1. Spell **heaviest.** Get ready. (Tap for each letter.) *H-E-A-V-I-E-S-T.*
- (Repeat for: **2. loneliness, 3. carrying, 4. copies, 5. denial, 6. fanciful.**)

Prompted Review

a. (Write on the board:)

> 1. children
> 2. claim
> 3. money
> 4. lengthen
> 5. value
> 6. glory
> 7. finally
> 8. informed

b. Word 1 is **children.** Spell **children.** Get ready. (Signal.) *C-H-I-L-D-R-E-N.*

c. Word 2 is **claim.** Spell **claim.** Get ready. (Signal.) *C-L-A-I-M.*

d. (Repeat step *c* for: **3. money, 4. lengthen, 5. value, 6. glory, 7. finally, 8. informed.**)

e. (Erase the board.)

• Now spell those words without looking.

f. Word 1 is **children.** Spell **children.** Get ready. (Signal.) *C-H-I-L-D-R-E-N.*

g. Word 2 is **claim.** Spell **claim.** Get ready. (Signal.) *C-L-A-I-M.*

h. (Repeat step *g* for: **3. money, 4. lengthen, 5. value, 6. glory, 7. finally, 8. informed.**)

i. (Give individual turns on **1. children, 2. claim, 3. money, 4. lengthen, 5. value, 6. glory, 7. finally, 8. informed.**)

EXERCISE 1

Morphographic Analysis

a. (Write on the board:)

> 1. describing = _____
>
> 2. preserve = _____
>
> 3. likeness = _____
>
> 4. misspelling = _____
>
> 5. frightening = _____

- Number your paper from 1 to 5. ✔
- Write the morphographs that go in each blank. Put plus signs between the morphographs. ✔

b. (Write to show:)

> 1. describing = de + scribe + ing
>
> 2. preserve = pre + serve
>
> 3. likeness = like + ness
>
> 4. misspelling = mis + spell + ing
>
> 5. frightening = fright + en + ing

c. Check your work. Make an **X** next to any item you got wrong. ✔

EXERCISE 2

Consonant-and-Y Rule

a. (Write on the board:)

> 1. vary + ed =
> 2. copy + er =
> 3. try + ed =
> 4. study + ing =
> 5. early + er =
> 6. carry + age =

b. Number your paper from 1 through 6. ✔
- Each of these words ends **consonant-and-y.**
- Copy the board on your paper with the plus and equal signs. ✔

c. Remember, when we add a morphograph to a word that ends **consonant-and-y,** we usually have to change the spelling of that word.
- Here is the rule: Change the **y** to **i** when the next morphograph begins with anything, except **i.**

d. (Point to the first **ed** on the board.)
- Does this suffix begin with an **i?** (Signal.) *No.*

e. The morphograph **e-d** does not begin with **i,** so we have to change the **y** to **i.**

f. Write **varied** after the equal sign for word 1. ✔

g. Finish the words on your own. ✔

h. Check your work. Make an **X** next to any word you got wrong.

i. Word 1. Spell **varied.** Get ready. (Tap for each letter.) *V-A-R-I-E-D.*

- (Repeat for: **2. copier, 3. tried, 4. studying, 5. earlier, 6. carriage.**)

EXERCISE 3

Spelling Review

> *Note:* Use context sentence for **main*.**

a. You're going to spell words.

b. Word 1 is **leave.** Spell **leave.** Get ready. (Signal.) *L-E-A-V-E.*

c. Word 2 is **main*.** Spell **main.** Get ready. (Signal.) *M-A-I-N.*

d. Word 3 is **boxes.** Spell **boxes.** Get ready. (Signal.) *B-O-X-E-S.*

e. Word 4 is **confront.** Spell **confront.** Get ready. (Signal.) *C-O-N-F-R-O-N-T.*

f. Word 5 is **inside.** Spell **inside.** Get ready. (Signal.) *I-N-S-I-D-E.*

g. Word 6 is **breathing.** Spell **breathing.** Get ready. (Signal.) *B-R-E-A-T-H-I-N-G.*

h. (Give individual turns on: **1. leave, 2. main, 3. boxes, 4. confront, 5. inside, 6. breathing.**)

EXERCISE 1

Word Introduction

a. (Write on the board:)

>   show
>   grow
>   low
>   flow
>   throw
>   blow
>   know

b. Get ready to read these words.
*   First word: **show.** What word? (Signal.)
    Show.
c. Next word: **grow.** What word? (Signal.)
    Grow.
*   (Repeat for: **low, flow, throw, blow, know.**)
d. Now spell those words.
*   Spell **show.** Get ready. (Signal.) *S-H-O-W.*
e. Spell **grow.** Get ready. (Signal.) *G-R-O-W.*
*   (Repeat for: **low, flow, throw, blow, know.**)
d. (Erase the board.)
*   Spell the words without looking.
g. Spell **show.** Get ready. (Signal.) *S-H-O-W.*
h. Spell **grow.** Get ready. (Signal.) *G-R-O-W.*
*   (Repeat for: **low, flow, throw, blow, know.**)

EXERCISE 2

Consonant-and-Y Rule

a. (Write on the board:)

>   1. cry + ing =
>
>   2. play + ful =
>
>   3. speedy + est =
>
>   4. story + es =
>
>   5. stay + ed =
>
>   6. worry + ing =

b. Number your paper from 1 through 6. ✔
*   Copy the board on your paper with the plus and equal signs. ✔
c. Some of these words follow the rule about changing a **y** to **i.** Do all the words on your own. ✔
d. Check your work. Make an **X** next to any word you got wrong.
e. Word 1. Spell **crying.** Get ready. (Tap for each letter.) *C-R-Y-I-N-G.*
*   (Repeat for: **2. playful, 3. speediest, 4. stories, 5. stayed, 6. worrying.**)

EXERCISE 3

Spelling Review

a. I'm going to spell either **listening, lengthen, lightest,** or **likable.**
b. Listen: **l-i-g-h-t-e-s-t.**
    What word? (Signal.) *Lightest.*
c. Listen: **l-e-n-g-t-h-e-n.**
    What word? (Signal.) *Lengthen.*
d. Listen: **l-i-s-t-e-n-i-n-g.**
    What word? (Signal.) *Listening.*
e. Listen: **l-i-k-a-b-l-e.**
    What word? (Signal.) *Likable.*
f. Get ready to spell those words.
g. Word 1. Spell **lightest.** Get ready. (Signal.) *L-I-G-H-T-E-S-T.*
h. Word 2. Spell **lengthen.** Get ready. (Signal.) *L-E-N-G-T-H-E-N.*
*   (Repeat step *h* for: **listening, likable.**)

EXERCISE 1

Word Building

a. (Write on the board:)

> 1. pre + serve + ing =
> 2. con + fuse + ed =
> 3. in + flame + ed =
> 4. con + serve =
> 5. gum + y =
> 6. de + fine + ing =

b. You're going to write the words that go after the equal signs.
- Some of these words follow the final **e** rule. Some follow the doubling rule. Be careful.
- Number your paper from 1 to 6. ✔

c. Word 1: Write **preserving** on your paper. ✔

d. Do the rest of the words on your own. ✔

e. Check your work. Make an **X** next to any word you got wrong.

f. Word 1. Spell **preserving**. Get ready. (Tap for each letter.) *P-R-E-S-E-R-V-I-N-G.*
- (Repeat for: **2. confused, 3. inflamed, 4. conserve, 5. gummy, 6. defining.**)

EXERCISE 2

Consonant-and-Y Rule

a. (Write on the board:)

> 1. worry + ed =
> 2. worry + ing =
> 3. baby + es =
> 4. worthy + ness =
> 5. fly + ing =
> 6. early + est =

b. Number your paper from 1 through 6. ✔
- Copy the board on your paper with the plus and equal signs. ✔

c. Some of these words follow the rule about changing a **y** to **i**. Do all the words on your own. ✔

d. Check your work. Make an **X** next to any word you got wrong.

e. Word 1. Spell **worried**. Get ready. (Tap for each letter.) *W-O-R-R-I-E-D.*
- (Repeat for: **2. worrying, 3. babies, 4. worthiness, 5. flying, 6. earliest.**)

EXERCISE 3

Prompted Review

a. (Write on the board:)

> 1. flow
> 2. frighten
> 3. remarkable
> 4. healthy
> 5. hopefully
> 6. throw
> 7. children
> 8. leave

b. Word 1 is **flow.** Spell **flow.** Get ready. (Signal.) *F-L-O-W.*

c. Word 2 is **frighten.** Spell **frighten.** Get ready. (Signal.) *F-R-I-G-H-T-E-N.*

d. (Repeat step c for: **3. remarkable, 4. healthy, 5. hopefully, 6. throw, 7. children, 8. leave.**)

e. (Erase the board.)
- Now spell those words without looking.

f. Word 1 is **flow.** Spell **flow.** Get ready. (Signal.) *F-L-O-W.*

g. Word 2 is **frighten.** Spell **frighten.** Get ready. (Signal.) *F-R-I-G-H-T-E-N.*

h. (Repeat step g for: **3. remarkable, 4. healthy, 5. hopefully, 6. throw, 7. children, 8. leave.**)

i. (Give individual turns on **1. flow, 2. frighten, 3. remarkable, 4. healthy, 5. hopefully, 6. throw, 7. children, 8. leave.**)

EXERCISE 1

Test

a. Today you have a spelling test. Number your lined paper from 1 through 10. ✔

b. Word 1 is **children.** What word? (Signal.) *Children.*

• Write the word **children.** ✔

c. Word 2 is **maddest.** What word? (Signal.) *Maddest.*

• Write the word **maddest.** ✔

d. (Repeat step c for: **3. notable, 4. frightful, 5. defining, 6. valuable, 7. stylish, 8. wrecked, 9. strengthen, 10. different.**)

e. Pick up your red pen. ✔
Make an **X** next to any word you spelled wrong.

• (Write on board:)

1. children	6. valuable
2. maddest	7. stylish
3. notable	8. wrecked
4. frightful	9. strengthen
5. defining	10. different

• Write the correct spelling next to any word you spelled wrong.
(Observe students and give feedback.)

EXERCISE 1

W as a Vowel Letter

a. (Write on the board:)

> **w**

b. **W** is usually a consonant letter, but sometimes it's a vowel letter.

c. Here is the rule: If **w** is at the end of a morphograph, then it is a vowel letter.

• Listen again: (Repeat the rule.)

d. (Write to show:)

> **w**
> 1. **throw**
> 2. **win**
> 3. **want**
> 4. **yellow**
> 5. **show**
> 6. **threw**

e. Number 1 is **throw**.
• Is the **w** a vowel letter or a consonant letter in the word **throw?**
• (Signal.) *A vowel letter.*
• How do you know? (Signal.) *It's at the end of a morphograph.*

f. Number 2 is **win**.
• Is the **w** a vowel letter or a consonant letter in the word **win?** (Signal.) *A consonant letter.*
• How do you know? (Signal.) *It's not at the end of a morphograph.*

g. Number 3 is **want**.
• Is the **w** a vowel letter or a consonant letter in the word **want?** (Signal.) *A consonant letter.*
• How do you know? (Signal.) *It's not at the end of a morphograph.*

h. Number 4 is **yellow**.
• Is the **w** a vowel letter or a consonant letter in the word **yellow?** (Signal.) *A vowel letter.*
• How do you know? (Signal.) *It's at the end of a morphograph.*

i. (Repeat step *h* for: **5. show, 6. threw.**)

EXERCISE 2

Morphographic Analysis

a. (Write on the board:)

> 1. **studied** = _____
> 2. **flying** = _____
> 3. **tried** = _____
> 4. **worried** = _____
> 5. **copies** = _____
> 6. **staying** = _____

• Number your paper from 1 to 6. ✔
• These words are made up of more than one morphograph. You're going to write the morphographs that go in each blank.

b. **Studied:** What's the first morphograph in **studied?** (Signal.) *Study.*

c. Item 1. Write **study** and a plus sign. Don't forget to write the **y** at the end of **study.** ✔

d. What's the next morphograph in **studied?** (Signal.) *E-D.*

e. Write **e-d.** ✔

f. Here are the morphographs for item 1.
• (Write to show:)

> 1. **studied = study + ed**

g. Do the rest of the words on your own. You have to write a **y** at the end of some of the morphographs. ✔

h. (Write to show:)

> 1. **studied = study + ed**
>
> 2. **flying = fly + ing**
>
> 3. **tried = try + ed**
>
> 4. **worried = worry + ed**
>
> 5. **copies = copy + es**
>
> 6. **staying = stay = ing**

• Check your work. Make an **X** next to any item you got wrong. ✔

Spelling Review

> *Note:* Use context sentence for **main***.

a. I'm going to spell some words. Listen carefully and tell me what word I spell.

b. Listen: **k-n-o-w.** What word? (Signal.) *Know.*

c. Listen: **f-i-n-a-l.** What word? (Signal.) *Final.*

d. (Repeat step *c* for: **boxing, context, main, throat.**)

e. Get ready to spell those words.

f. Word 1. Spell **know.** Get ready. (Signal.) *K-N-O-W.*

g. Word 2. Spell **final.** Get ready. (Signal.) *F-I-N-A-L.*

h. (Repeat step *g* for: **3. boxing, 4. context, 5. main*, 6. throat.**)

LESSON 42

EXERCISE 1

Sentence

a. (Write on the board:)

> **Whose turn is it to move?**

- I'll read the sentence on the board: **Whose turn is it to move?**
- Let's spell some of those words.

b. Spell **Whose**. Get ready. (Signal.) *W-H-O-S-E.*
- Spell **turn**. Get ready. (Signal.) *T-U-R-N.*
- Spell **move**. Get ready. (Signal.) *M-O-V-E.*

c. Copy this sentence on lined paper. (Observe students and give feedback.)

d. Read the sentence you just copied. Get ready. (Signal.) *Whose turn is it to move?*

EXERCISE 2

Word Introduction

a. (Write on the board:)

> spray
> text
> ruin
> fluid
> govern
> treat

b. Get ready to read these words.
- First word: **spray**. What word? (Signal.) *Spray.*

c. Next word: **text**. What word? (Signal.) *Text.*
- (Repeat for: **ruin, fluid, govern, treat.**)

d. Now spell those words.
- Spell **spray**. Get ready. (Signal.) *S-P-R-A-Y.*

e. Spell **text**. Get ready. (Signal.) *T-E-X-T.*
- (Repeat for: **ruin, fluid, govern, treat.**)

f. (Erase the board.)
- Spell the words without looking.

g. Spell **spray**. Get ready. (Signal.) *S-P-R-A-Y.*

h. Spell **text**. Get ready. (Signal.) *T-E-X-T.*
- (Repeat for: **ruin, fluid, govern, treat.**)

EXERCISE 3

Spelling Review

a. You're going to write words.
- Number your paper 1 to 6. ✔

b. Word 1 is **worrier**. Write it. ✔

c. Word 2 is **throw**. Write it. ✔

d. (Repeat step c for: **3. fanciest, 4. strengthening, 5. conserve, 6. unfriendly.**)

e. Check your work. Make an **X** next to any word you got wrong.

f. Word 1. Spell **worrier**. Get ready. (Tap for each letter.) *W-O-R-R-I-E-R.*

- (Repeat for: **2. throw, 3. fanciest, 4. strengthening, 5. conserve, 6. unfriendly.**)

EXERCISE 1

Sentence

a. (Write on the board:)

> **Whose turn is it to move?**

- I'll read the sentence on the board: **Whose turn is it to move?**
- Let's spell some of those words.

b. Spell **Whose.** Get ready. (Signal.) *W-H-O-S-E.*
- Spell **turn.** Get ready. (Signal.) *T-U-R-N.*
- Spell **move.** Get ready. (Signal.) *M-O-V-E.*

c. (Erase the board.)

d. Now let's spell some of the words in that sentence without looking.
- Spell **Whose.** Get ready. (Signal.) *W-H-O-S-E.*
- Spell **turn.** Get ready. (Signal.) *T-U-R-N.*
- Spell **move.** Get ready. (Signal.) *M-O-V-E.*

EXERCISE 2

Word Building

a. (Write on the board:)

> 1. re + sign + ing =
> 2. happy + ness =
> 3. un + pack + ed =
> 4. play + ful + ness =
> 5. float + s =
> 6. in + value + able =

b. You're going to write the words that go after the equal signs.
- Some of these words follow the final **e** rule. Some follow the **y-to i** rule. Be careful.
- Number your paper from 1 to 6. ✔

c. Word 1: Write **resigning** on your paper. ✔

d. Do the rest of the words on your own. ✔

e. Check your work. Make an **X** next to any word you got wrong.

f. Word 1. Spell **resigning.** Get ready. (Tap for each letter.) *R-E-S-I-G-N-I-N-G.*
- (Repeat for: **2. happiness, 3. unpacked, 4. playfulness, 5. floats, 6. invaluable.**)

EXERCISE 3

Prompted Review

a. (Write on the board:)

> 1. carried
> 2. govern
> 3. treated
> 4. blower
> 5. denial
> 6. children

b. Word 1 is **carried.** Spell **carried.** Get ready. (Signal.) *C-A-R-R-I-E-D.*

c. Word 2 is **govern.** Spell **govern.** Get ready. (Signal.) *G-O-V-E-R-N.*

d. (Repeat step c for: **3. treated, 4. blower, 5. denial, 6. children.**)

e. (Erase the board.)
- Now spell those words without looking.

f. Word 1 is **carried.** Spell **carried.** Get ready. (Signal.) *C-A-R-R-I-E-D.*

g. Word 2 is **govern.** Spell **govern.** Get ready. (Signal.) *G-O-V-E-R-N.*

h. (Repeat step g for: **3. treated, 4. blower, 5. denial, 6. children.**)

i. (Give individual turns on: **1. carried, 2. govern, 3. treated, 4. blower, 5. denial, 6. children.**)

LESSON 44

EXERCISE 1

Sentence

a. (Write on the board:)

> **Whose turn is it to move?**

- I'll read the sentence on the board: **Whose turn is it to move?**
- Let's spell some of those words.

b. Spell **Whose.** Get ready. (Signal.) *W-H-O-S-E.*
- Spell **turn.** Get ready. (Signal.) *T-U-R-N.*
- Spell **move.** Get ready. (Signal.) *M-O-V-E.*

c. (Erase the board.)

d. Now let's spell some of the words in that sentence without looking.
- Spell **Whose.** Get ready. (Signal.) *W-H-O-S-E.*
- Spell **turn.** Get ready. (Signal.) *T-U-R-N.*
- Spell **move.** Get ready. (Signal.) *M-O-V-E.*

EXERCISE 2

Morphographic Analysis

a. (Write on the board:)

> 1. studied = _____
> 2. likable = _____
> 3. madness = _____
> 4. playful = _____
> 5. snapping = _____
> 6. hoping = _____

- Number your paper from 1 to 6. ✔

b. You're going to write the morphographs that go in each blank.
- Remember, write the morphographs the way they're spelled. You might have to add an **e** to a word or "undouble" a word, or change an **i** back into a **y.**

c. Do the words on your own. ✔

d. (Write to show:)

> 1. studied = study + ed
> 2. likable = like + able
> 3. madness = mad + ness
> 4. playful = play + ful
> 5. snapping = snap + ing
> 6. hoping = hope + ing

- Check your work. Make an **X** next to any item you got wrong. ✔

EXERCISE 3

Spelling Review

a. I'm going to spell some words. Listen carefully and tell me what word I spell.

b. Listen: **t-e-x-t.** What word? (Signal.) *Text.*

c. Listen: **t-r-e-a-t.** What word? (Signal.) *Treat.*

d. (Repeat step c for: **yellow, growing, lightly, fanciest.**)

e. Get ready to spell those words.

f. Word 1. Spell **text.** Get ready. (Signal.) *T-E-X-T.*

g. Word 2. Spell **treat.** Get ready. (Signal.) *T-R-E-A-T.*

h. (Repeat step g for: **3. yellow, 4. growing, 5. lightly, 6. fanciest.**)

Lesson 44 **57**

LESSON 45

EXERCISE 1

Sentence

a. You're going to write this sentence: **Whose turn is it to move?**

b. Say the sentence. Get ready. (Signal.) *Whose turn is it to move?*

c. Write the sentence. ✔

d. (Write on the board:)

> **Whose turn is it to move?**

e. Check your work. Make an **X** next to any word you got wrong. ✔

EXERCISE 2

Word Building

a. (Write on the board:)

> 1. sleep + y + ness =
> 2. fine + al + ly =
> 3. in + form + al =
> 4. re + place + ment =
> 5. pre + serve + ing =
> 6. mis + judge + ed =

b. You're going to write the words that go after the equal signs.

• Some of these words follow the final **e** rule. Some follow the **y-to-i** rule. Be careful.

• Number your paper from 1 to 6. ✔

c. Word 1: Write **sleepiness** on your paper. ✔

d. Do the rest of the words on your own. ✔

e. Check your work. Make an **X** next to any word you got wrong.

f. Word 1. Spell **sleepiness**. Get ready. (Tap for each letter.) S-L-E-E-P-I-N-E-S-S.

• (Repeat for: **2. finally, 3. informal, 4. replacement, 5. preserving, 6. misjudged.**)

EXERCISE 3

Spelling Review

a. You're going to spell words.

b. Word 1 is **playfully**. Spell **playfully**. Get ready. (Signal.) *P-L-A-Y-F-U-L-L-Y.*

c. Word 2 is **worried**. Spell **worried**. Get ready. (Signal.) *W-O-R-R-I-E-D.*

d. Word 3 is **showing**. Spell **showing**. Get ready. (Signal.) *S-H-O-W-I-N-G.*

e. Word 4 is **worthiest**. Spell **worthiest**. Get ready. (Signal.) *W-O-R-T-H-I-E-S-T.*

f. Word 5 is **finally**. Spell **finally**. Get ready. (Signal.) *F-I-N-A-L-L-Y.*

g. Word 6 is **grabbed**. Spell **grabbed**. Get ready. (Signal.) *G-R-A-B-B-E-D.*

h. (Give individual turns on: **1. playfully, 2. worried, 3. showing, 4. worthiest, 5. finally, 6. grabbed.**)

LESSON 46

EXERCISE 1

Word Introduction

a. (Write on the board:)

> cause
> pause
> poison
> strange

b. Get ready to read these words.
- First word: **cause.** What word? (Signal.) *Cause.*
c. Next word: **pause.** What word? (Signal.) *Pause.*
- (Repeat for: **poison, strange.**)
d. Now spell those words.
- Spell **cause.** Get ready. (Signal.) *C-A-U-S-E.*
e. Spell **pause.** Get ready. (Signal.) *P-A-U-S-E.*
- (Repeat for: **poison, strange.**)
f. (Erase the board.)
- Spell the words without looking.
g. Spell **cause.** Get ready. (Signal.) *C-A-U-S-E.*
h. Spell **pause.** Get ready. (Signal.) *P-A-U-S-E.*
- (Repeat for: **poison, strange.**)
i. Get ready to write those words.
j. Word 1: **pause.** Write it. ✔
- (Repeat for: **2. strange, 3. poison, 4. cause.**)

EXERCISE 2

Word Building

a. (Write on the board:)

> 1. re + turn + ing =
> 2. re + move + able =
> 3. shop + er =
> 4. con + serve + ing =
> 5. hope + less + ness =
> 6. re + mark + able =
> 7. govern + ing =

b. You're going to write the words that go after the equal signs.
- Some of these words follow the final **e** rule. Some follow the doubling rule. Be careful.
- Number your paper from 1 to 7. ✔
c. Word 1: Write **returning** on your paper. ✔
d. Do the rest of the words on your own. ✔
e. Check your work. Make an **X** next to any word you got wrong.
f. Word 1. Spell **returning.** Get ready. (Tap for each letter.) *R-E-T-U-R-N-I-N-G.*
- (Repeat for: **2. removable, 3. shopper, 4. conserving, 5. hopelessness, 6. remarkable, 7. governing.**)

EXERCISE 3

Prompted Review

a. (Write on the board:)

> 1. removing
> 2. signals
> 3. prescribe
> 4. unlikely
> 5. mistaken
> 6. fluidly

b. Word 1 is **removing.** Spell **removing.** Get ready. (Signal.) *R-E-M-O-V-I-N-G.*
c. Word 2 is **signals.** Spell **signals.** Get ready. (Signal.) *S-I-G-N-A-L-S.*
d. (Repeat step *c* for: **3. prescribe, 4. unlikely, 5. mistaken, 6. fluidly.**)
e. (Erase the board.)
- Now spell those words without looking.
f. Word 1 is **removing.** Spell **removing.** Get ready. (Signal.) *R-E-M-O-V-I-N-G.*
g. Word 2 is **signals.** Spell **signals.** Get ready. (Signal.) *S-I-G-N-A-L-S.*
h. (Repeat step *g* for: **3. prescribe, 4. unlikely, 5. mistaken, 6. fluidly.**)
i. (Give individual turns on: **1. removing, 2. signals, 3. prescribe, 4. unlikely, 5. mistaken, 6. fluidly.**)

LESSON 47

EXERCISE 1

S and ES

a. (Write on the board:)

> 1. study + es = studies
> 2. try + es = tries
> 3. carry + es = carries
> 4. worry + es = worries

b. When a word ends **consonant-and-y,** you change the **y** to **i** and add **e-s,** not **s.**

c. Word 1: Spell **studies.** Get ready. (Signal.) *S-T-U-D-I-E-S.*

d. Word 2: Spell **tries.** Get ready. (Signal.) *T-R-I-E-S.*

e. Word 3: Spell **carries.** Get ready. (Signal.) *C-A-R-R-I-E-S.*

f. Word 4: Spell **worries.** Get ready. (Signal.) *W-O-R-R-I-E-S.*

g. Remember, just use your **y-to-i** rule, and add **e-s,** not **s.**

EXERCISE 2

Morphographic Analysis

a. (Write on the board:)

> 1. usable = _____
>
> 2. lonely = _____
>
> 3. contested = _____
>
> 4. furry = _____
>
> 5. foolishness = _____
>
> 6. catches = _____

- Number your paper from 1 to 6. ✔
- Write the morphographs that go in each blank. Put plus signs between the morphographs. ✔

b. (Write to show:)

> 1. usable = use + able
>
> 2. lonely = lone + ly
>
> 3. contested = con + test + ed
>
> 4. furry = fur + y
>
> 5. foolishness = fool + ish + ness
>
> 6. catches = catch + es

c. Check your work. Make an **X** next to any item you got wrong. ✔

EXERCISE 3

Sentence Variations

a. Get ready to write on lined paper.
- You are going to write a sentence made up of words you know how to spell. Put the right end mark at the end of the sentence.

b. The sentence is: **Whose books are the heaviest?**
- Say that sentence. Get ready. (Signal.) *Whose books are the heaviest?*
- (Repeat step *b* until firm.)

c. Write it on your paper. ✔

d. (Write on the board:)

> **Whose books are the heaviest?**

e. Check your work. Make an **X** next to any word you got wrong. ✔

LESSON 48

EXERCISE 1

Affix Introduction

a. (Write on the board:)

> 1. govern + ment =
> 2. treat + ment =
> 3. move + ment =

- All these words have the morphograph **ment**.
b. Number your paper from 1 to 3. ✔
c. Add the morphographs together. Write just the new words. ✔
d. Check your work. Make an **X** next to any word you got wrong.
e. Word 1. Spell **government**. Get ready. (Tap for each letter.) *G-O-V-E-R-N-M-E-N-T.*
- (Repeat for: **2. treatment, 3. movement.**)

EXERCISE 2

Sentence Variations

a. Get ready to write on lined paper.
- You are going to write a sentence made up of words you know how to spell. Put the right end mark at the end of the sentence.
b. The sentence is: **His sleepiness worried the children.**
- Say that sentence. Get ready. (Signal.) *His sleepiness worried the children.*
- (Repeat step *b* until firm.)
c. Write it on your paper. ✔
d. (Write on the board:)

> **His sleepiness worried the children.**

e. Check your work. Make an **X** next to any word you got wrong. ✔

EXERCISE 3

Prompted Review

a. (Write on the board:)

> 1. governing
> 2. stranger
> 3. showing
> 4. studied
> 5. strange
> 6. pause

b. Word 1 is **governing**. Spell **governing**. Get ready. (Signal.) *G-O-V-E-R-N-I-N-G.*
c. Word 2 is **stranger**. Spell **stranger**. Get ready. (Signal.) *S-T-R-A-N-G-E-R.*
d. (Repeat step *c* for: **3. showing, 4. studied, 5. strange, 6. pause.**)
e. (Erase the board.)
- Now spell those words without looking.
f. Word 1 is **governing**. Spell **governing**. Get ready. (Signal.) *G-O-V-E-R-N-I-N-G.*
g. Word 2 is **stranger**. Spell **stranger**. Get ready. (Signal.) *S-T-R-A-N-G-E-R.*
h. (Repeat step *g* for: **3. showing, 4. studied, 5. strange, 6. pause.**)
i. (Give individual turns on: **1. governing, 2. stranger, 3. showing, 4. studied, 5. strange, 6. pause.**)

Lesson 48 **61**

LESSON 49

EXERCISE 1

Affix Introduction
a. (Write on the board:)

> 1. de + press =
> 2. de + serve =
> 3. de + sign =

- All these words have the morphograph **de.**
b. Number your paper from 1 to 3. ✔
c. Add the morphographs together. Write just the new words. ✔
d. Check your work. Make an **X** next to any word you got wrong.
e. Word 1. Spell **depress.** Get ready. (Tap for each letter.) D-E-P-R-E-S-S.
- (Repeat for: **2. deserve, 3. design.**)

EXERCISE 2

Word Building
a. (Write on the board:)

> 1. govern + ment =
> 2. de + light + ful =
> 3. re + strict + ed =
> 4. mis + take + en =
> 5. lone + ly + ness =
> 6. self + ish + ly =

b. You're going to write the words that go after the equal signs.
- Some of these words follow the final **e** rule. Some follow the **y-to-i** rule. Be careful.
- Number your paper from 1 to 6. ✔
c. Word 1: Write **government** on your paper. ✔
d. Do the rest of the words on your own. ✔
e. Check your work. Make an **X** next to any word you got wrong.
f. Word 1. Spell **government.** Get ready. (Tap for each letter.) G-O-V-E-R-N-M-E-N-T.
- (Repeat for: **2. delightful, 3. restricted, 4. mistaken, 5. loneliness, 6. selfishly.**)

EXERCISE 3

> *Note:* Use a context sentence for **whose*.**

Spelling Review
a. Get ready to spell and write some words.
b. Word 1 is **cause.**
- What word? (Signal.) *Cause.*
- Spell **cause.** Get ready. (Signal.) C-A-U-S-E.
- Write it. ✔
c. Word 2 is **poison.**
- What word? (Signal.) *Poison.*
- Spell **poison.** Get ready. (Signal.) P-O-I-S-O-N.
- Write it. ✔
d. (Repeat step c for: **3. whose*, 4. fluidly, 5. valuable, 6. lengthening.**)
e. I'll spell each word.
- Put an **X** next to any word you missed and write that word correctly.
- (Spell each word twice. Write the words on the board as you spell them.)

1. cause	4. fluidly
2. poison	5. valuable
3. whose	6. lengthening

LESSON 50

EXERCISE 1

Note: In step e, students will need a red pen (or colored pencil).

Test

a. Today you have a spelling test. Number your lined paper from 1 through 10. ✔

b. Word 1 is **stranger.** What word? (Signal.) *Stranger.*

- Write the word **stranger.** ✔

c. Word 2 is **govern.** What word? (Signal.) *Govern.*

- Write the word **govern.** ✔

d. (Repeat step *c* for: **3. movement, 4. preserve, 5. mistaken, 6. spotless, 7. undrinkable, 8. groaning, 9. thoughtful, 10. stretcher.)**

e. Pick up your red pen. ✔
Make an **X** next to any word you spelled wrong.

- (Write on board:)

1. stranger	6. spotless
2. govern	7. undrinkable
3. movement	8. groaning
4. preserve	9. thoughtful
5. mistaken	10. stretcher

- Write the correct spelling next to any word you spelled wrong.
(Observe students and give feedback.)

EXERCISE 1

Word Introduction

> *Note:* Pronounce the sound /ā/ like the letter name **A**.

a. (Write on the board:)

> brain
> chain
> drain
> gain
> rain
> sprain
> stain

b. Get ready to read these words.
- In each of these words, the sound /ā/ is spelled **a-i.**
- First word: **brain.** What word? (Signal.) *Brain.*
c. Next word: **chain.** What word? (Signal.) *Chain.*
- (Repeat for: **drain, gain, rain, sprain, stain.**)
d. Now spell those words.
- Spell **brain.** Get ready. (Signal.) *B-R-A-I-N.*
e. Spell **chain.** Get ready. (Signal.) *C-H-A-I-N.*
- (Repeat for: **drain, gain, rain, sprain, stain.**)
f. (Erase the board.)
- Spell the words without looking.
g. Spell **brain.** Get ready. (Signal.) *B-R-A-I-N.*
h. Spell **chain.** Get ready. (Signal.) *C-H-A-I-N.*
- (Repeat for: **drain, gain, rain, sprain, stain.**)

EXERCISE 2

Word Building
a. (Write on the board:)

> 1. de + sign + er =
> 2. con + fine + ing
> 3. de + part + ment =
> 4. pre + wrap + ed =
> 5. re + place + ment =
> 6. rain + y + est =

b. You're going to write the words that go after the equal signs.
- Some of these words follow the final **e** rule. Some follow the doubling rule or the **y-to-i** rule. Be careful.
- Number your paper from 1 to 6. ✔
c. Word 1: Write **designer** on your paper. ✔
d. Do the rest of the words on your own. ✔
e. Check your work. Make an **X** next to any word you got wrong.
f. Word 1. Spell **designer.** Get ready. (Tap for each letter.) *D-E-S-I-G-N-E-R.*
- (Repeat for: **2. confining, 3. department, 4. prewrapped, 5. replacement, 6. rainiest.**)

EXERCISE 3

Spelling Review
a. Get ready to spell and write some words.
b. Word 1 is **choices.**
- What word? (Signal.) *Choices.*
- Spell **choices.** Get ready. (Signal.) *C-H-O-I-C-E-S.*
- Write it. ✔
c. Word 2 is **differently.**
- What word? (Signal.) *Differently.*
- Spell **differently.** Get ready. (Signal.) *D-I-F-F-E-R-E-N-T-L-Y.*
- Write it. ✔
d. (Repeat step c for: **3. thoughtful, 4. stretcher.**)
e. I'll spell each word.
- Put an **X** next to any word you missed and write that word correctly.
- (Spell each word twice. Write the words on the board as you spell them.)

> 1. choices   3. thoughtful
> 2. differently   4. stretcher

LESSON 52

Morphographic Analysis

a. You're going to tell me the morphographs in words, and then you're going to spell those words.
- **Design:** What's the first morphograph in **design?** (Signal.) *De.*
- Next morphograph? (Signal.) *Sign.* Yes, **sign.**
- Spell **design.** Get ready. (Signal.) *D-E-S-I-G-N.*

b. **Replayed:** What's the first morphograph in **replayed?** (Signal.) *Re.*
- Next morphograph? (Signal.) *Play.*
- Next morphograph? (Signal.) *E-D.*
- Spell **replayed.** Get ready. (Signal.) *R-E-P-L-A-Y-E-D.*

c. **Usable:** What's the first morphograph in **usable?** (Signal.) *Use.*
- Next morphograph? (Signal.) *Able.*
- Spell **usable.** Get ready. (Signal.) *U-S-A-B-L-E.*

d. **Unlikely:** What's the first morphograph in **unlikely?** (Signal.) *Un.*
- Next morphograph? (Signal.) *Like.*
- Next morphograph? (Signal.) *Ly.*
- Spell **unlikely.** Get ready. (Signal.) *U-N-L-I-K-E-L-Y.*

e. **Previewing:** What's the first morphograph in **previewing?** (Signal.) *Pre.*
- Next morphograph? (Signal.) *View.*
- Next morphograph? (Signal.) *Ing.*
- Spell **previewing.** Get ready. (Signal.) *P-R-E-V-I-E-W-I-N-G.*

f. **Misprinted:** What's the first morphograph in **misprinted?** (Signal.) *Mis.*
- Next morphograph? (Signal.) *Print.*
- Next morphograph? (Signal.) *E-D.*
- Spell **misprinted.** Get ready. (Signal.) *M-I-S-P-R-I-N-T-E-D.*

Word Building

a. (Write on the board:)

> 1. lone + ly + ness =
> 2. care + ful + ly =
> 3. de + light + ful =
> 4. author + ing =
> 5. self + ish + ly =
> 6. point + less =
> 7. fancy + est =
> 8. con + fine + ing =

b. You're going to write the words that go after the equal signs.
- Some of these words follow the final **e** rule. Some follow the **y-to-i** rule. Be careful.
- Number your paper from 1 to 8. ✔
c. Word 1: Write **loneliness** on your paper. ✔
d. Do the rest of the words on your own. ✔
e. Check your work. Make an **X** next to any word you got wrong.
f. Word 1. Spell **loneliness.** Get ready. (Tap for each letter.) *L-O-N-E-L-I-N-E-S-S.*
- (Repeat for: **2. carefully, 3. delightful, 4. authoring, 5. selfishly, 6. pointless, 7. fanciest, 8. confining.**)

Prompted Review

a. (Write on the board:)

> 1. sprain
> 2. poison
> 3. raining
> 4. strangely
> 5. invaluable
> 6. contests

b. Word 1 is **sprain.** Spell **sprain.** Get ready.
(Signal.) *S-P-R-A-I-N.*

c. Word 2 is **poison.** Spell **poison.** Get ready.
(Signal.) *P-O-I-S-O-N.*

d. (Repeat step *c* for: **3. raining, 4. strangely,
5. invaluable, 6. contests.**)

e. (Erase the board.)

• Now spell those words without looking.

f. Word 1 is **sprain.** Spell **sprain.** Get ready.
(Signal.) *S-P-R-A-I-N.*

g. Word 2 is **poison.** Spell **poison.** Get ready.
(Signal.) *P-O-I-S-O-N.*

h. (Repeat step *g* for: **3. raining, 4. strangely,
5. invaluable, 6. contests.**)

i. (Give individual turns on: **1. sprain,
2. poison, 3. raining, 4. strangely,
5. invaluable, 6. contests.**)

EXERCISE 1

Morphographic Analysis

a. (Write on the board:)

> 1. studied = _____
>
> 2. voltage = _____
>
> 3. foolishly = _____
>
> 4. removal = _____
>
> 5. dosage = _____
>
> 6. confirmed = _____

- Number your paper from 1 to 6. ✔
- Write the morphographs that go in each word. Put plus signs between the morphographs. ✔

b. (Write to show:)

> 1. studied = study + ed
>
> 2. voltage = volt + age
>
> 3. foolishly = fool +ish + ly
>
> 4. removal = re = move + al
>
> 5. dosage = dose + age
>
> 6. confirmed = con + firm + ed

c. Check your work. Make an **X** next to any item you got wrong. ✔

EXERCISE 2

Sentence Variations

a. Get ready to write on lined paper.
- You are going to write a sentence made up of words you know how to spell. Put the right end mark at the end of the sentence.

b. The sentence is: **He foolishly remained in a different place.**
- Say that sentence. Get ready. (Signal.) *He foolishly remained in a different place.*
- (Repeat step *b* until firm.)

c. Write it. ✔

d. Get ready to check your spelling. Put an **X** next to any word you missed.

e. Spell **He.** Get ready. (Signal.) *H-E.*
- Check it. ✔

f. Spell **foolishly.** Get ready. (Signal.) *F-O-O-L-I-S-H-L-Y.*
- Check it. ✔
- (Repeat step *f* for: **remained, in, a, different, place.**)

g. What end mark did you put at the end of the sentence? (Signal.) *A period.*
- Check it. ✔

h. Fix any words you missed.

EXERCISE 3

Spelling Review

a. You're going to spell words.

b. Word 1 is **fancier.** Spell **fancier.** Get ready. (Signal.) *F-A-N-C-I-E-R.*

c. Word 2 is **loneliness.** Spell **loneliness.** Get ready. (Signal.) *L-O-N-E-L-I-N-E-S-S.*

d. Word 3 is **hurries.** Spell **hurries.** Get ready. (Signal.) *H-U-R-R-I-E-S.*

e. Word 4 is **listening.** Spell **listening.** Get ready. (Signal.) *L-I-S-T-E-N-I-N-G.*

f. Word 5 is **preschool.** Spell **preschool.** Get ready. (Signal.) *P-R-E-S-C-H-O-O-L.*

g. Word 6 is **regrowing.** Spell **regrowing.** Get ready. (Signal.) *R-E-G-R-O-W-I-N-G.*

h. (Give individual turns on: **1. fancier, 2. loneliness, 3. hurries, 4. listening, 5. preschool, 6. regrowing.**)

EXERCISE 1

Contractions

> **Note:** The two words of a contraction are written on the board together in this exercise. For example, **wasnot** is written for **was not,** in order to show students how contractions work.

a. (Write on the board:)

wasnot	**heis**
youwill	**hasnot**
shouldnot	**itis**

- Listen: A contraction is made from two words, and a contraction has a part missing.

b. (Point to **wasnot.**)
- The contraction of **was not** is **wasn't.**
- (Erase the **o.**)

wasn t
youwill
shouldnot

- The missing part in **wasn't** is **o.** We show that the part is missing with an apostrophe.
- (Make an apostrophe in place of the **o.**)

wasn't
youwill
shouldnot

c. (Point to **youwill.**)
- The contraction of **you will** is **you'll.**
- What's the missing part in **you'll?** (Signal.) *W-I.*
- (Erase the **w-i.**)

wasn't
you ll
shouldnot

- What mark goes in place of **w-i?** (Signal.) *An apostrophe.*

- (Make an apostrophe.)

wasn't
you'll
shouldnot

d. (Point to **shouldnot.**)
- The contraction of **should not** is **shouldn't.**
- What's the missing part in **shouldn't?** (Signal.) *o.*
(Erase the second **o.**)

wasn't
you'll
shouldn t

- What mark goes in place of **o?** (Signal.) *An apostrophe.*
- (Make an apostrophe.)

wasn't
you'll
shouldn't

e. (Repeat step *d* for: **heis, hasnot, itis.**)
- (The board begins:)

wasn't	**heis**
you'll	**hasnot**
shouldn't	**itis**

- (The board ends:)

wasn't	**he's**
you'll	**hasn't**
shouldn't	**it's**

f. (Erase the board.)
- My turn to spell **wasn't**: w-a-s-n-apostrophe-t.
g. Your turn: Spell **wasn't.** Get ready. (Signal.) *W-A-S-N-apostrophe-T.*
h. Spell **hasn't.** Get ready. (Signal.) *H-A-S-N-apostrophe-T.*
- (Repeat for: **he's, shouldn't, you'll, it's.**)

Word Building

a. (Write on the board:)

> 1. cloud + y + ness =
> 2. stain + ed =
> 3. snap + ing =
> 4. strange + er =
> 5. length + en + ing =
> 6. early + est =

b. You're going to write the words that go after the equal signs.

- Some of these words follow the final **e** rule. Some follow the doubling rule or the **y-to-i** rule. Be careful.
- Number your paper from 1 to 6. ✔

c. Word 1: Write **cloudiness** on your paper. ✔

d. Do the rest of the words on your own. ✔

e. Check your work. Make an **X** next to any word you got wrong.

f. Word 1. Spell **cloudiness.** Get ready. (Tap for each letter.) *C-L-O-U-D-I-N-E-S-S.*

- (Repeat for: **2. stained, 3. snapping, 4. stranger, 5. lengthening, 6. earliest.**)

Spelling Review

a. You're going to spell words.

b. Word 1 is **consented.** Spell **consented.** Get ready. (Signal.) *C-O-N-S-E-N-T-E-D.*

c. Word 2 is **selfishness.** Spell **selfishness.** Get ready. (Signal.) *S-E-L-F-I-S-H-N-E-S-S.*

d. Word 3 is **unequally.** Spell **unequally.** Get ready. (Signal.) *U-N-E-Q-U-A-L-L-Y.*

e. Word 4 is **signals.** Spell **signals.** Get ready. (Signal.) *S-I-G-N-A-L-S.*

f. Word 5 is **catches.** Spell **catches.** Get ready. (Signal.) *C-A-T-C-H-E-S.*

g. Word 6 is **misspends.** Spell **misspends.** Get ready. (Signal.) *M-I-S-S-P-E-N-D-S.*

h. (Give individual turns on: **1. consented, 2. selfishness, 3. unequally, 4 signals, 5. catches, 6. misspends.**)

LESSON 55

EXERCISE 1

Contractions

> *Note:* The two words of a contraction are written on the board together in this exercise. For example, **wouldnot** is written for **would not**, in order to show students how contractions work.

a. (Write on the board:)

wouldnot	cannot
wehave	lhave
weare	theyare

- Listen: A contraction is made from two words, and a contraction has a part missing.

b. (Point to **wouldnot.**)
- The contraction of **would not** is **wouldn't.**
- (Erase the second **o.**)

> wouldn t
> wehave
> weare

- The missing part in **wouldn't** is **o.** We show that the part is missing with an apostrophe.
- (Make an apostrophe in place of the **o.**)

> wouldn't
> wehave
> weare

c. (Point to **wehave.**)
- The contraction of **we have** is **we've.**
- What's the missing part in **we've?** (Signal.) *H-A.*
- (Erase the **h-a.**)

> wouldn't
> we ve
> weare

- What mark goes in place of **h-a?** (Signal.) *An apostrophe.*
- (Make an apostrophe.)

> wouldn't
> we've
> weare

d. (Point to **weare.**)
- The contraction of **we are** is **we're.**
- What's the missing part in **we're?** (Signal.) *A.*
- (Erase the **a.**)

> wouldn't
> we've
> we re

- What mark goes in place of **a?** (Signal.) *An apostrophe.*
- (Make an apostrophe.)

> wouldn't
> we've
> we're

e. (Repeat step *d* for: **cannot, lhave, theyare.**)
- (The board begins:)

> cannot
> lhave
> theyare

- (The board ends:)

> can't
> I've
> they're

f. (Erase the board.)
- My turn to spell **wouldn't**: w-o-u-l-d-n-apostrophe-t.
g. Your turn: Spell **wouldn't.** Get ready. (Signal.) *W-O-U-L-D-N-apostrophe-T.*
h. Spell **I've.** Get ready. (Signal.) *I-apostrophe-V-E.*
- (Repeat for: **can't, we're, we've, they're.**)

70   *Lesson 55*

Morphographic Analysis

a. (Write on the board:)

> 1. playfully = _____
>
> 2. strangeness = _____
>
> 3. global = _____
>
> 4. rebuildable = _____
>
> 5. dripping = _____
>
> 6. stylish = _____

- Number your paper from 1 to 6. ✔
b. There are three morphographs in **playfully.** The last morphograph is **ly.**
- Write the morphographs that go in each blank. Put plus signs between the morphographs. ✔
c. (Write to show:)

> 1. playfully = play = ful + ly
>
> 2. strangeness = strange + ness
>
> 3. global = globe + al
>
> 4. rebuildable = re + build + able
>
> 5. dripping = drip + ing
>
> 6. stylish = style + ish

d. Check your work. Make an **X** next to any item you got wrong. ✔

Prompted Review

a. (Write on the board:)

> 1. lengthening
> 2. straightest
> 3. designer
> 4. maddening
> 5. cloudiness
> 6. replacement

b. Word 1 is **lengthening.** Spell **lengthening.** Get ready. (Signal.) *L-E-N-G-T-H-E-N-I-N-G.*

c. Word 2 is **straightest.** Spell **straightest.** Get ready. (Signal.) *S-T-R-A-I-G-H-T-E-S-T.*

d. (Repeat step c for: **3. designer, 4. maddening, 5. cloudiness, 6. replacement.**)

e. (Erase the board.)

- Now spell those words without looking.

f. Word 1 is **lengthening.** Spell **lengthening.** Get ready. (Signal.) *L-E-N-G-T-H-E-N-I-N-G.*

g. Word 2 is **straightest.** Spell **straightest.** Get ready. (Signal.) *S-T-R-A-I-G-H-T-E-S-T.*

h. (Repeat step g for: **3. designer, 4. maddening, 5. cloudiness, 6. replacement.**)

i. (Give individual turns on: **1. lengthening, 2. straightest, 3. designer, 4. maddening, 5. cloudiness, 6. replacement.**)

LESSON 56

EXERCISE 1

Sentence

a. (Write on the board:)

> **Our yellow flowers bloomed early.**

- I'll read the sentence on the board: **Our yellow flowers bloomed early.**
- Let's spell those words.

b. Spell **Our.** Get ready. (Signal.) *O-U-R.*
- Spell **yellow.** Get ready. (Signal.) *Y-E-L-L-O-W.*
- Spell **flowers.** Get ready. (Signal.) *F-L-O-W-E-R-S.*
- Spell **bloomed.** Get ready. (Signal.) *B-L-O-O-M-E-D.*
- Spell **early.** Get ready. (Signal.) *E-A-R-L-Y.*

c. Copy this sentence on lined paper. (Observe students and give feedback.)

d. Read the sentence you just copied. Get ready. (Signal.) *Our yellow flowers bloomed early.*

EXERCISE 2

Contractions

> *Note:* Beginning in this lesson, an apostrophe is shown in student responses for contractions.

a. (Write on the board:)

> **1. should not =**
> **2. it is =**
> **3. we have =**
> **4. he is =**
> **5. you will =**
> **6. they are =**

b. (Point to **should not.**)
- Tell me the contraction for **should not.** Get ready. (Signal.) *Shouldn't.*
- Spell **shouldn't.** Get ready. (Signal.) *S-H-O-U-L-D-N-'-T.*

c. (Point to **it is.**)
- Tell me the contraction for **it is.** Get ready. (Signal.) *It's.*
- Spell **it's.** Get ready. (Signal.) *I-T-'-S.*

d. (Repeat step *c* for: **3. we have, we've 4. he is, he's 5. you will, you'll 6. they are, they're.**)

EXERCISE 3

Spelling Review

a. Get ready to spell and write some words.

b. Word 1 is **poisoning.**
- What word? (Signal.) *Poisoning.*
- Spell **poisoning.** Get ready. (Signal.) *P-O-I-S-O-N-I-N-G.*
- Write it. ✔

c. Word 2 is **govern.**
- What word? (Signal.) *Govern.*
- Spell **govern.** Get ready. (Signal.) *G-O-V-E-R-N.*
- Write it. ✔

d. (Repeat step *c* for: **3. children, 4. studied.**)

e. I'll spell each word.
- Put an **X** next to any word you missed and write that word correctly.
- (Spell each word twice. Write the words on the board as you spell them.)

> **1. poisoning   3. children**
> **2. govern   4. studied**

EXERCISE 1

Sentence

a. (Write on the board:)

> **Our yellow flowers bloomed early.**

- I'll read the sentence on the board: **Our yellow flowers bloomed early.**
- Let's spell those words.

b. Spell **Our.** Get ready. (Signal.) *O-U-R.*
- Spell **yellow.** Get ready. (Signal.) *Y-E-L-L-O-W.*
- Spell **flowers.** Get ready. (Signal.) *F-L-O-W-E-R-S.*
- Spell **bloomed.** Get ready. (Signal.) *B-L-O-O-M-E-D.*
- Spell **early.** Get ready. (Signal.) *E-A-R-L-Y.*

c. (Erase the board.)

d. Now let's spell the words in that sentence without looking.
- Spell **our.** Get ready. (Signal.) *O-U-R.*
e. Spell **yellow.** Get ready. (Signal.) *Y-E-L-L-O-W.*
- (Repeat for: **flowers, bloomed, early.**)

EXERCISE 2

Word Building

a. (Write on the board:)

> 1. fate + al + ly =
> 2. con + fine + ment =
> 3. drain + age =
> 4. spin + er + s =
> 5. sleep + y + ness =
> 6. taste + ful + ly =

b. You're going to write the words that go after the equal signs.
- Some of these words follow the final **e** rule. Some follow the doubling rule or **y-to-i** rule. Be careful.
- Number your paper from 1 to 6. ✔

c. Word 1: Write **fatally** on your paper. ✔

d. Do the rest of the words on your own. ✔

e. Check your work. Make an **X** next to any word you got wrong.

f. Word 1. Spell **fatally.** Get ready. (Tap for each letter.) *F-A-T-A-L-L-Y.*
- (Repeat for: **2. confinement, 3. drainage, 4. spinners, 5. sleepiness, 6. tastefully.**)

EXERCISE 3

Spelling Review

a. You're going to spell words.

b. Word 1 is **prescribed.** Spell **prescribed.** Get ready. (Signal.) *P-R-E-S-C-R-I-B-E-D.*

c. Word 2 is **unfriendly.** Spell **unfriendly.** Get ready. (Signal.) *U-N-F-R-I-E-N-D-L-Y.*

d. Word 3 is **confusing.** Spell **confusing.** Get ready. (Signal.) *C-O-N-F-U-S-I-N-G.*

e. Word 4 is **carrier.** Spell **carrier.** Get ready. (Signal.) *C-A-R-R-I-E-R.*

f. Word 5 is **spinning.** Spell **spinning.** Get ready. (Signal.) *S-P-I-N-N-I-N-G.*

g. Word 6 is **deserving.** Spell **deserving.** Get ready. (Signal.) *D-E-S-E-R-V-I-N-G.*

h. (Give individual turns on: **1. prescribed, 2. unfriendly, 3. confusing, 4. carrier, 5. spinning, 6. deserving.**)

EXERCISE 1

Sentence

a. (Write on the board:)

Our yellow flowers bloomed early.

- I'll read the sentence on the board: **Our yellow flowers bloomed early.**
- Let's spell those words.

b. Spell **Our.** Get ready. (Signal.) *O-U-R.*
- Spell **yellow.** Get ready. (Signal.) *Y-E-L-L-O-W.*
- Spell **flowers.** Get ready. (Signal.) *F-L-O-W-E-R-S.*
- Spell **bloomed.** Get ready. (Signal.) *B-L-O-O-M-E-D.*
- Spell **early.** Get ready. (Signal.) *E-A-R-L-Y.*

c. (Erase the board.)

d. Now let's spell the words in that sentence without looking.
- Spell **Our.** Get ready. (Signal.) *O-U-R.*
e. Spell **yellow.** Get ready. (Signal.) *Y-E-L-L-O-W.*
- (Repeat for: **flowers, bloomed, early.**)

EXERCISE 2

Contractions

Note: An apostrophe is shown in student responses for contractions.

a. (Write on the board:)

1. I am =
2. she will =
3. should not =
4. has not =
5. they will =
6. you are =

b. (Point to **I am.**)
- Tell me the contraction for **I am.** Get ready. (Signal.) *I'm.*
- Spell **I'm.** Get ready. (Signal.) *I-'-M.*

c. (Point to **she will.**)
- Tell me the contraction for **she will.** Get ready. (Signal.) *She'll.*
- Spell **she'll.** Get ready. (Signal.) *S-H-E-'-L-L.*

d. (Repeat step c for: **3. should not, shouldn't 4. has not, hasn't 5. they will, they'll 6. you are, you're.**)

EXERCISE 3

Sentence Variations

a. Get ready to write on lined paper.
- You are going to write a sentence made up of words you know how to spell. Put the right end mark at the end of the sentence.

b. The sentence is: **The wreckage was frightening and maddening.**
- Say that sentence. Get ready. (Signal.) *The wreckage was frightening and maddening.*
- (Repeat step *b* until firm.)

c. Write it. ✔

d. Get ready to check your spelling. Put an **X** next to any word you missed.

e. Spell **The.** Get ready. (Signal.) *T-H-E.*
- Check it. ✔

f. Spell **wreckage.** Get ready. (Signal.) *W-R-E-C-K-A-G-E.*
- Check it. ✔
- (Repeat step *f* for: **was, frightening, and, maddening.**)

g. What end mark did you put at the end of the sentence? (Signal.) *A period.*
- Check it. ✔

h. Fix any words you missed.

LESSON 59

EXERCISE 1

Sentence

a. You're going to write this sentence: **Our yellow flowers bloomed early.**

b. Say the sentence. Get ready. (Signal.) *Our yellow flowers bloomed early.*

c. Write the sentence. ✔

d. (Write on the board:)

> **Our yellow flowers bloomed early.**

e. Check your work. Make an **X** next to any word you got wrong. ✔

EXERCISE 2

Morphographic Analysis

a. (Write on the board:)

> 1. finally = _____
>
> 2. summed = _____
>
> 3. inflaming = _____
>
> 4. hurried = _____
>
> 5. unbreakable = _____
>
> 6. remaining = _____

- Number your paper from 1 to 6. ✔
- Write the morphographs that go in each blank. Put plus signs between the morphographs. ✔

b. (Write to show:)

> 1. finally = fine + al + ly
>
> 2. summed = sum + ed
>
> 3. inflaming = in + flame + ing
>
> 4. hurried = hurry + ed
>
> 5. unbreakable = un + break + able
>
> 6. remaining = re + main + ing

c. Check your work. Make an **X** next to any item you got wrong. ✔

EXERCISE 3

Prompted Review

a. (Write on the board:)

> 1. shouldn't
> 2. drainage
> 3. government
> 4. breathe
> 5. boyish
> 6. safer
> 7. barred
> 8. luckily

b. Word 1 is **shouldn't**. Spell **shouldn't**. Get ready. (Signal.) *S-H-O-U-L-D-N-'-T.*

c. Word 2 is **drainage**. Spell **drainage**. Get ready. (Signal.) *D-R-A-I-N-A-G-E.*

d. (Repeat step *c* for: **3. government, 4. breathe, 5. boyish, 6. safer, 7. barred, 8. luckily.**)

e. (Erase the board.)

- Now spell those words without looking.

f. Word 1 is **shouldn't**. Spell **shouldn't**. Get ready. (Signal.) *S-H-O-U-L-D-N-'-T.*

g. Word 2 is **drainage**. Spell **drainage**. Get ready. (Signal.) *D-R-A-I-N-A-G-E.*

h. (Repeat step *g* for: **3. government, 4. breathe, 5. boyish, 6. safer, 7. barred, 8. luckily.**)

i. (Give individual turns on: **1. shouldn't, 2. drainage, 3. government, 4. breathe, 5. boyish, 6. safer, 7. barred, 8. luckily.**)

EXERCISE 1

Test

a. Today you have a spelling test. Number your lined paper from 1 through 10. ✔

b. Word 1 is **rainy.** What word? (Signal.) *Rainy.*
- Write the word **rainy.** ✔

c. Word 2 is **couldn't.** What word? (Signal.) *Couldn't.*
- Write the word **couldn't.** ✔

d. (Repeat step *c* for: **3. sleepiness, 4. studies, 5. sketchy, 6. driving, 7. inflame, 8. preserving, 9. hotter, 10. heavy.**)

e. Pick up your red pen. ✔
Make an **X** next to any word you spelled wrong.

- (Write on the board:)

1. rainy	6. driving
2. couldn't	7. inflame
3. sleepiness	8. preserving
4. studies	9. hotter
5. sketchy	10. heavy

- Write the correct spelling next to any word you spelled wrong.
(Observe students and give feedback.)

EXERCISE 1

Sentence

a. (Write on the board:)

> **Carrying the heavy load is sure to make me breathe hard.**

- I'll read the sentence on the board: **Carrying the heavy load is sure to make me breathe hard.**
- Let's spell some of those words.

b. Spell **Carrying.** Get ready. (Signal.) *C-A-R-R-Y-I-N-G.*

- Spell **heavy.** Get ready. (Signal.) *H-E-A-V-Y.*
- Spell **load.** Get ready. (Signal.) *L-O-A-D.*
- Spell **sure.** Get ready. (Signal.) *S-U-R-E.*
- Spell **breathe.** Get ready. (Signal.) *B-R-E-A-T-H-E.*

c. Copy this sentence on lined paper. (Observe students and give feedback.)

d. Read the sentence you just copied. Get ready. (Signal.) *Carrying the heavy load is sure to make me breathe hard.*

EXERCISE 2

Morphographic Analysis

a. (Write on the board:)

> 1. wrapper = _____
>
> 2. strengthening = _____
>
> 3. sturdier = _____
>
> 4. preschools = _____
>
> 5. describing = _____
>
> 6. investment = _____

- Number your paper from 1 to 6. ✔
- Write the morphographs that go in each blank. Put plus signs between the morphographs. ✔

b. (Write to show:)

> 1. wrapper = wrap + er
>
> 2. strengthening = strength + en + ing
>
> 3. sturdier = sturdy + er
>
> 4. preschools = pre + school + s
>
> 5. describing = de + scribe + ing
>
> 6. investment = in + vest + ment

c. Check your work. Make an **X** next to any item you got wrong. ✔

EXERCISE 3

Spelling Review

> *Note:* Use a context sentence for **they're***.

a. You're going to spell words.

b. Word 1 is **they're***. Spell **they're.** Get ready. (Signal.) *T-H-E-Y-'-R-E.*

c. Word 2 is **loneliness.** Spell **loneliness.** Get ready. (Signal.) *L-O-N-E-L-I-N-E-S-S.*

d. Word 3 is **maddening.** Spell **maddening.** Get ready. (Signal.) *M-A-D-D-E-N-I-N-G.*

e. Word 4 is **government.** Spell **government.** Get ready. (Signal.) *G-O-V-E-R-N-M-E-N-T.*

f. Word 5 is **sleepiest.** Spell **sleepiest.** Get ready. (Signal.) *S-L-E-E-P-I-E-S-T.*

g. Word 6 is **resigned.** Spell **resigned.** Get ready. (Signal.) *R-E-S-I-G-N-E-D.*

h. (Give individual turns on: **1. they're, 2. loneliness, 3. maddening, 4. government, 5. sleepiest, 6. resigned.**)

EXERCISE 1

Sentence

a. (Write on the board:)

> **Carrying the heavy load is sure to make me breathe hard.**

- I'll read the sentence on the board: **Carrying the heavy load is sure to make me breathe hard.**
- Let's spell some of those words.

b. Spell **Carrying.** Get ready. (Signal.) *C-A-R-R-Y-I-N-G.*

- Spell **heavy.** Get ready. (Signal.) *H-E-A-V-Y.*
- Spell **load.** Get ready. (Signal.) *L-O-A-D.*
- Spell **sure.** Get ready. (Signal.) *S-U-R-E.*
- Spell **breathe.** Get ready. (Signal.) *B-R-E-A-T-H-E.*

EXERCISE 2

Affix Introduction

a. (Write on the board:)

> **1. ex + port =
> 2. ex + press =
> 3. ex + change =**

- All these words have the morphograph **ex.**

b. Number your paper from 1 to 3. ✔

c. Add the morphographs together. Write just the new words. ✔

d. Check your work. Make an **X** next to any word you got wrong.

e. Word 1. Spell **export.** Get ready. (Tap for each letter.) *E-X-P-O-R-T.*

- (Repeat for: **2. express, 3. exchange.**)

EXERCISE 3

Spelling Review

a. You're going to spell words.

b. Word 1 is **couldn't.** Spell **couldn't.** Get ready. (Signal.) *C-O-U-L-D-N-'-T.*

c. Word 2 is **passages.** Spell **passages.** Get ready. (Signal.) *P-A-S-S-A-G-E-S.*

d. Word 3 is **fancier.** Spell **fancier.** Get ready. (Signal.) *F-A-N-C-I-E-R.*

e. Word 4 is **earliest.** Spell **earliest.** Get ready. (Signal.) *E-A-R-L-I-E-S-T.*

f. Word 5 is **children.** Spell **children.** Get ready. (Signal.) *C-H-I-L-D-R-E-N.*

g. Word 6 is **different.** Spell **different.** Get ready. (Signal.) *D-I-F-F-E-R-E-N-T.*

h. (Give individual turns on: **1. couldn't, 2. passages, 3. fancier, 4. earliest, 5. children, 6. different.**)

LESSON 63

EXERCISE 1

Sentence

a. (Write on the board:)

> **Carrying the heavy load is sure to make me breathe hard.**

- I'll read the sentence on the board: **Carrying the heavy load is sure to make me breathe hard.**
- Let's spell some of those words.

b. Spell **Carrying.** Get ready. (Signal.) *C-A-R-R-Y-I-N-G.*

- Spell **heavy.** Get ready. (Signal.) *H-E-A-V-Y.*
- Spell **load.** Get ready. (Signal.) *L-O-A-D.*
- Spell **sure.** Get ready. (Signal.) *S-U-R-E.*
- Spell **breathe.** Get ready. (Signal.) *B-R-E-A-T-H-E.*

EXERCISE 2

Busyness and Business

a. (Write on the board:)

> **busyness**
> **business**

b. (Point to **busyness.**)

- This word is pronounced **bizz-ee-ness.** What word? (Signal.) *Busyness.*

c. (Point to **business.**)

- This word is pronounced **bizz-ness.** What word? (Signal.) *Business.*

d. (Direct students to read **busyness** and **business** until firm.)

e. **Busyness** does not follow the rule about changing **y** to **i. Business** does follow the rule.

f. Does **business** follow the rule about changing **y** to **i?** (Signal.) *Yes.*

- Yes. **Business** follows the rule. Remember that.

EXERCISE 3

Spelling Review

a. Get ready to spell and write some words.

b. Word 1 is **bloomed.**

- What word? (Signal.) *Bloomed.*
- Spell **bloomed.** Get ready. (Signal.) *B-L-O-O-M-E-D.*
- Write it. ✔

c. Word 2 is **can't.**

- What word? (Signal.) *Can't.*
- Spell **can't.** Get ready. (Signal.) *C-A-N-'-T.*
- Write it. ✔

d. (Repeat step c for: **3. cloudiness, 4. instilled, 5. confronted, 6. thankfully, 7. misshaped, 8. signal.**)

e. I'll spell each word.

- Put an **X** next to any word you missed and write that word correctly.
- (Spell each word twice. Write the words on the board as you spell them.)

1. bloomed	5. confronted
2. can't	6. thankfully
3. cloudiness	7. misshaped
4. instilled	8. signal

EXERCISE 1

Sentence

a. You're going to write this sentence:
Carrying the heavy load is sure to make me breathe hard.

b. Say the sentence. Get ready. (Signal.)
Carrying the heavy load is sure to make me breathe hard.

c. Write the sentence. ✔

d. (Write on the board:)

> **Carrying the heavy load is sure to make me breathe hard.**

e. Check your work. Make an **X** next to any word you got wrong. ✔

EXERCISE 2

Word Building

a. (Write on the board:)

> 1. ex + cite + ing =
> 2. con + sign + ment =
> 3. in + cure + able =
> 4. in + form + er =
> 5. pre + plan + ed =
> 6. room + y + er =

b. You're going to write the words that go after the equal signs.

• Some of these words follow the final **e** rule. Some follow the doubling rule or the **y-to-i** rule. Be careful.

• Number your paper from 1 to 6. ✔

c. Word 1: Write **exciting** on your paper. ✔

d. Do the rest of the words on your own. ✔

e. Check your work. Make an **X** next to any word you got wrong.

f. Word 1. Spell **exciting.** Get ready. (Tap for each letter.) *E-X-C-I-T-I-N-G.*

• (Repeat for: **2. consignment, 3. incurable, 4. informer, 5. preplanned, 6. roomier.**)

EXERCISE 3

Prompted Review

a. (Write on the board:)

> 1. business
> 2. busyness
> 3. flowers
> 4. showing
> 5. heaviest
> 6. we're

b. Word 1 is **business.** Spell **business.** Get ready. (Signal.) *B-U-S-I-N-E-S-S.*

c. Word 2 is **busyness.** Spell **busyness.** Get ready. (Signal.) *B-U-S-Y-N-E-S-S.*

d. (Repeat step c for: **3. flowers, 4. showing, 5. heaviest, 6. we're.**)

e. (Erase the board.)

• Now spell those words without looking.

f. Word 1 is **business.** Spell **business.** Get ready. (Signal.) *B-U-S-I-N-E-S-S.*

g. Word 2 is **busyness.** Spell **busyness.** Get ready. (Signal.) *B-U-S-Y-N-E-S-S.*

h. (Repeat step g for: **3. flowers, 4. showing, 5. heaviest, 6. we're.**)

i. (Give individual turns on: **1. business, 2. busyness, 3. flowers, 4. showing, 5. heaviest, 6. we're.**)

LESSON 65

EXERCISE 1

Sentence Variations

a. Get ready to write on lined paper.
- You are going to write a sentence made up of words you know how to spell. Put the right end mark at the end of the sentence.

b. The sentence is: **Those lights need sturdier wrapping.**
- Say that sentence. Get ready. (Signal.) *Those lights need sturdier wrapping.*
- (Repeat step *b* until firm.)

c. Write it. ✔

d. Get ready to check your spelling. Put an **X** next to any word you missed.

e. Spell **Those.** Get ready. (Signal.) *T-H-O-S-E.*
- Check it. ✔

f. Spell **lights.** Get ready. (Signal.) *L-I-G-H-T-S.*
- Check it. ✔
- (Repeat step *f* for: **need, sturdier, wrapping.**)

g. What end mark did you put at the end of the sentence? (Signal.) *A period.*
- Check it. ✔

h. Fix any words you missed.

EXERCISE 2

Word Building

a. (Write on the board:)

> 1. con + sign + ment =
> 2. mis + quote + ed =
> 3. pre + date + ed =
> 4. re + tract + ed =
> 5. un + re + cover + ed =
> 6. de + press + ing =

b. You're going to write the words that go after the equal signs.
- Some of these words follow the final **e** rule. Be careful.
- Number your paper from 1 to 6. ✔

c. Word 1: Write **consignment** on your paper. ✔

d. Do the rest of the words on your own. ✔

e. Check your work. Make an **X** next to any word you got wrong.

f. Word 1. Spell **consignment.** Get ready. (Tap for each letter.) *C-O-N-S-I-G-N-M-E-N-T.*
- (Repeat for: **2. misquoted, 3. predated, 4. retracted, 5. unrecovered, 6. depressing.**)

EXERCISE 3

Prompted Review

a. (Write on the board:)

> 1. breathe
> 2. breathing
> 3. business
> 4. exchanging
> 5. hasn't
> 6. strangely

b. Word 1 is **breathe.** Spell **breathe.** Get ready. (Signal.) *B-R-E-A-T-H-E.*

c. Word 2 is **breathing.** Spell **breathing.** Get ready. (Signal.) *B-R-E-A-T-H-I-N-G.*

d. (Repeat step *c* for: **3. business, 4. exchanging, 5. hasn't, 6. strangely.**)

e. (Erase the board.)
- Now spell those words without looking.

f. Word 1 is **breathe.** Spell **breathe.** Get ready. (Signal.) *B-R-E-A-T-H-E.*

g. Word 2 is **breathing.** Spell **breathing.** Get ready. (Signal.) *B-R-E-A-T-H-I-N-G.*

h. (Repeat step *g* for: **3. business, 4. exchanging, 5. hasn't, 6. strangely.**)

i. (Give individual turns on: **1. breathe, 2. breathing, 3. business, 4. exchanging, 5. hasn't, 6. strangely.**)

LESSON 66

EXERCISE 1

Word Introduction

a. (Write on the board:)

> **quick**
> **quiz**
> **quest**

b. Get ready to read these words.
- First word: **quick.** What word? (Signal.) *Quick.*
c. Next word: **quiz.** What word? (Signal.) *Quiz.*
- (Repeat for: **quest.**)
d. Now spell those words.
- Spell **quick.** Get ready. (Signal.) *Q-U-I-C-K.*
e. Spell **quiz.** Get ready. (Signal.) *Q-U-I-Z.*
- (Repeat for: **quest.**)
f. (Erase the board.)
- Spell the words without looking.
g. Spell **quick.** Get ready. (Signal.) *Q-U-I-C-K.*
h. Spell **quiz.** Get ready. (Signal.) *Q-U-I-Z.*
- (Repeat for: **quest.**)
i. Get ready to write those words.
j. Word 1: **quiz.** Write it. ✔
- (Repeat for: **2. quest, 3. quick.**)

EXERCISE 2

Morphographic Analysis

a. You're going to tell me the morphographs in words, and then you're going to spell those words.
- **Exporter:** What's the first morphograph in **exporter?** (Signal.) *Ex.*
- Next morphograph? (Signal.) *Port.*
- Next morphograph? (Signal.) *Er.*
- Spell **exporter.** Get ready. (Signal.) *E-X-P-O-R-T-E-R.*
b. **Contest:** What's the first morphograph in **contest?** (Signal.) *Con.*
- Next morphograph? (Signal.) *Test.*
- Spell **contest.** Get ready. (Signal.) *C-O-N-T-E-S-T.*
c. **Sleepy:** What's the first morphograph in **sleepy?** (Signal.) *Sleep.*
- Next morphograph? (Signal.) *Y.*
- Spell **sleepy.** Get ready. (Signal.) *S-L-E-E-P-Y.*

d. **Informal:** What's the first morphograph in **informal?** (Signal.) *In.*
- Next morphograph? (Signal.) *Form.*
- Next morphograph? (Signal.) *Al.*
- Spell **informal.** Get ready. (Signal.) *I-N-F-O-R-M-A-L.*
e. **Misspending:** What's the first morphograph in **misspending?** (Signal.) *Mis.*
- Next morphograph? (Signal.) *Spend.*
- Next morphograph? (Signal.) *Ing.*
- Spell **misspending.** Get ready. (Signal.) *M-I-S-S-P-E-N-D-I-N-G.*
f. **Contest:** What's the first morphograph in **contest?** (Signal.) *Con.*
- Next morphograph? (Signal.) *Test.*
- Spell **contest.** Get ready. (Signal.) *C-O-N-T-E-S-T.*

EXERCISE 3

Spelling Review

a. Get ready to spell and write some words.
b. Word 1 is **load.**
- What word? (Signal.) *Load.*
- Spell **load.** Get ready. (Signal.) *L-O-A-D.*
- Write it. ✔
c. Word 2 is **maddened.**
- What word? (Signal.) *Maddened.*
- Spell **maddened.** Get ready. (Signal.) *M-A-D-D-E-N-E-D.*
- Write it. ✔
d. (Repeat step c for: **3. girlishly, 4. unbreakable, 5. starring, 6. poison.**)
e. I'll spell each word.
- Put an **X** next to any word you missed and write that word correctly.
- (Spell each word twice. Write the words on the board as you spell them.)

> 1. **load**   4. **unbreakable**
> 2. **maddened**   5. **starring**
> 3. **girlishly**   6. **poison**

EXERCISE 1

Sentence Variations

a. Get ready to write on lined paper.
- You are going to write a sentence made up of words you know how to spell. Put the right end mark at the end of the sentence.

b. The sentence is: **The judge was delighted with the lucky painter.**
- Say that sentence. Get ready. (Signal.) *The judge was delighted with the lucky painter.*
- (Repeat step *b* until firm.)

c. Write it. ✔

d. Get ready to check your spelling. Put an **X** next to any word you missed.

e. Spell **The.** Get ready. (Signal.) *T-H-E.*
- Check it. ✔

f. Spell **judge.** Get ready. (Signal.) *J-U-D-G-E.*
- Check it. ✔
- (Repeat step *f* for: **was, delighted, with, the, lucky, painter.**)

g. What end mark did you put at the end of the sentence? (Signal.) *A period.*
- Check it. ✔

h. Fix any words you missed.

EXERCISE 2

Word Building

> *Note:* Pronounce /kw/ like the first sounds in **<u>quiz</u>**: /<u>kw</u>iz/.

a. (Write on the board:)

```
1. quiz + ing =

2. quit + er =

3. heavy + est =

4. ex + change + ing =

5. force + ful + ly =

6. un + break + able =

7. volt + age + es =

8. re + quest =
```

b. You're going to write the words that go after the equal signs.
- Some of these words follow the final **e** rule or the **y-to-i** rule.

c. Two of these words follow the doubling rule.
- (Write to show:)

```
       c c v c
1. q u i z + ing =
       c c v c
2. q u i t + er =
```

- Listen: **quiz,** /kwiz/. The letters **q-u** make the same sound as **k-w**: /kw/. **Q-u-i-z** ends **c-v-c,** so we follow the doubling rule.
- (Write to show:)

```
       c c v c
1. q u i z + ing = quizzing
       c c v c
2. q u i t + er =
```

d. Word 1. Spell **quizzing.** Get ready. (Signal.) *Q-U-I-Z-Z-I-N-G.*
- Word 2. Spell **quitter.** Get ready. (Signal.) *Q-U-I-T-T-E-R.* Yes, **q-u-i-t-t-e-r.**

e. Number your paper from 1 to 8. ✔

f. Word 1: Write **quizzing** on your paper. ✔

g. Do the rest of the words on your own. ✔

h. Check your work. Make an **X** next to any word you got wrong.

i. Word 1. Spell **quizzing.** Get ready. (Tap for each letter.) *Q-U-I-Z-Z-I-N-G.*
- (Repeat for: **2. quitter, 3. heaviest, 4. exchanging, 5. forcefully, 6. unbreakable, 7. voltages, 8. request.**)

Spelling Review

a. You're going to spell words.

b. Word 1 is **expressed.** Spell **expressed.**
    Get ready. (Signal.) *E-X-P-R-E-S-S-E-D.*

c. Word 2 is **loaded.** Spell **loaded.** Get ready.
    (Signal.) *L-O-A-D-E-D.*

d. Word 3 is **carried.** Spell **carried.** Get ready.
    (Signal.) *C-A-R-R-I-E-D.*

e. Word 4 is **surely.** Spell **surely.** Get ready.
    (Signal.) *S-U-R-E-L-Y.*

f. (Give individual turns on: **1. expressed,
    2. loaded, 3. carried, 4. surely.**)

EXERCISE 1

Word Introduction

> *Note:* Use a context sentence for **cite***.

a. (Write on the board:)

> tract
> cite
> found
> vest
> tend
> tense

b. Get ready to read these words.
- First word: **tract.** What word? (Signal.) *Tract.*

c. Next word: **cite*.** What word? (Signal.) *Cite.*
- (Repeat for: **found, vest, tend, tense.**)

d. Now spell those words.
- Spell **tract.** Get ready. (Signal.) *T-R-A-C-T.*

e. Spell **cite.** Get ready. (Signal.) *C-I-T-E.*
- (Repeat for: **found, vest, tend, tense.**)

f. (Erase the board.)
- Spell the words without looking.

g. Spell **tract.** Get ready. (Signal.) *T-R-A-C-T.*

h. Spell **cite*.** Get ready. (Signal.) *C-I-T-E.*
- (Repeat for: **found, vest, tend, tense.**)

EXERCISE 2

Word Building

a. (Write on the board:)

> 1. in + sure + ing =
> 2. ex + cite + ing =
> 3. de + serve + ing =
> 4. worry + er =
> 5. thought + ful + ly =
> 6. sleep + y + ness =

b. You're going to write the words that go after the equal signs.
- Some of these words follow the final **e** rule. Some follow the **y-to-i** rule. Be careful.
- Number your paper from 1 to 6. ✔

c. Word 1: Write **insuring** on your paper. ✔

d. Do the rest of the words on your own. ✔

e. Check your work. Make an **X** next to any word you got wrong.

f. Word 1. Spell **insuring.** Get ready. (Tap for each letter.) *I-N-S-U-R-I-N-G.*
- (Repeat for: **2. exciting, 3. deserving, 4. worrier, 5. thoughtfully, 6. sleepiness.**)

EXERCISE 3

Prompted Review

a. (Write on the board:)

> 1. quickly
> 2. helplessness
> 3. foolishly
> 4. constricting
> 5. quizzes
> 6. hardest

b. Word 1 is **quickly.** Spell **quickly.** Get ready. (Signal.) *Q-U-I-C-K-L-Y.*

c. Word 2 is **helplessness.** Spell **helplessness.** Get ready. (Signal.) *H-E-L-P-L-E-S-S-N-E-S-S.*

d. (Repeat step *c* for: **3. foolishly, 4. constricting, 5. quizzes, 6. hardest.**)

e. (Erase the board.)
- Now spell those words without looking.

f. Word 1 is **quickly.** Spell **quickly.** Get ready. (Signal.) *Q-U-I-C-K-L-Y.*

g. Word 2 is **helplessness.** Spell **helplessness.** Get ready. (Signal.) *H-E-L-P-L-E-S-S-N-E-S-S.*

h. (Repeat step *g* for: **3. foolishly, 4. constricting, 5. quizzes, 6. hardest.**)

i. (Give individual turns on: **1. quickly, 2. helplessness, 3. foolishly, 4. constricting, 5. quizzes, 6. hardest.**)

EXERCISE 1

Sentence Variations

a. Get ready to write on lined paper.
- You are going to write a sentence made up of words you know how to spell. Put the right end mark at the end of the sentence.
b. The sentence is: **Make sketches to go with the stories.**
- Say that sentence. Get ready. (Signal.) *Make sketches to go with the stories.*
- (Repeat step *b* until firm.)
c. Write it. ✔
d. Get ready to check your spelling. Put an **X** next to any word you missed.
e. Spell **Make.** Get ready. (Signal.) *M-A-K-E.*
- Check it. ✔
f. Spell **sketches.** Get ready. (Signal.) *S-K-E-T-C-H-E-S.*
- Check it. ✔
- (Repeat step *f* for: **to, go, with, the, stories.**)
g. What end mark did you put at the end of the sentence? (Signal.) *A period.*
- Check it. ✔
h. Fix any words you missed.

EXERCISE 2

Morphographic Analysis

a. (Write on the board:)

    1. invested = _____

    2. pretend = _____

    3. quickness = _____

    4. insure = _____

    5. extract = _____

    6. contracted = _____

- Number your paper from 1 to 6. ✔
- Write the morphographs that go in each blank. Put plus signs between the morphographs. ✔

b. (Write to show:)

    1. invested = in + vest + ed

    2. pretend = pre + tend

    3. quickness = quick + ness

    4. insure = in + sure

    5. extract = ex + tract

    6. contracted = con + tract + ed

c. Check your work. Make an **X** next to any item you got wrong. ✔

EXERCISE 3

Spelling Review

a. You're going to spell words.
b. Word 1 is **unfounded.** Spell **unfounded.** Get ready. (Signal.) *U-N-F-O-U-N-D-E-D.*
c. Word 2 is **request.** Spell **request.** Get ready. (Signal.) *R-E-Q-U-E-S-T.*
d. Word 3 is **express.** Spell **express.** Get ready. (Signal.) *E-X-P-R-E-S-S.*
e. Word 4 is **conserve.** Spell **conserve.** Get ready. (Signal.) *C-O-N-S-E-R-V-E.*
f. Word 5 is **pitifully.** Spell **pitifully.** Get ready. (Signal.) *P-I-T-I-F-U-L-L-Y.*
g. Word 6 is **flatten.** Spell **flatten.** Get ready. (Signal.) *F-L-A-T-T-E-N.*
h. (Give individual turns on: **1. unfounded, 2. request, 3. express, 4. conserve, 5. pitifully, 6. flatten.**)

LESSON 70

EXERCISE 1

> *Note:* In step e, students will need a red pen
> (or colored pencil).

Test

a. Today you have a spelling test. Number
your lined paper from 1 through 10. ✔

b. Word 1 is **business.** What word? (Signal.)
Business.

- Write the word **business.** ✔

c. Word 2 is **earlier.** What word? (Signal.)
Earlier.

- Write the word **earlier.** ✔

d. (Repeat step *c* for: **3. breathing,
4. flattest, 5. hasn't, 6. pretend, 7. heavy,
8. carried, 9. bloomed, 10. sprained.**)

e. Pick up your red pen. ✔
Make an **X** next to any word you spelled
wrong.

- (Write on board:)

1. business	6. pretend
2. earlier	7. heavy
3. breathing	8. carried
4. flattest	9. bloomed
5. hasn't	10. sprained

- Write the correct spelling next to any word
you spelled wrong.
(Observe students and give feedback.)

EXERCISE 1

Sentence

a. (Write on the board:)

> **One athlete finished the contest before everyone else.**

- I'll read the sentence on the board: **One athlete finished the contest before everyone else.**
- Let's spell some of those words.

b. Spell **athlete**. Get ready. (Signal.) *A-T-H-L-E-T-E.*

- Spell **finished**. Get ready. (Signal.) *F-I-N-I-S-H-E-D.*
- Spell **contest**. Get ready. (Signal.) *C-O-N-T-E-S-T.*
- Spell **before**. Get ready. (Signal.) *B-E-F-O-R-E.*
- Spell **everyone**. Get ready. (Signal.) *E-V-E-R-Y-O-N-E.*

c. Copy this sentence on lined paper. (Observe students and give feedback.)

d. Read the sentence you just copied. Get ready. (Signal.) *One athlete finished the contest before everyone else.*

EXERCISE 2

Word Building

a. (Write on the board:)

> 1. re + tract + ing =
> 2. ex + cite + ed =
> 3. pre + tend + ing =
> 4. tense + ly =
> 5. pack + age + es =
> 6. carry + ed =

b. You're going to write the words that go after the equal signs.

- Some of these words follow the final **e** rule. Some follow the **y-to-i** rule. Be careful.
- Number your paper from 1 to 6. ✔

c. Word 1: Write **retracting** on your paper. ✔

d. Do the rest of the words on your own. ✔

e. Check your work. Make an **X** next to any word you got wrong.

f. Word 1. Spell **retracting**. Get ready. (Tap for each letter.) *R-E-T-R-A-C-T-I-N-G.*

- (Repeat for: **2. excited, 3. pretending, 4. tensely, 5. packages, 6. carried.**)

EXERCISE 3

Spelling Review

a. You're going to spell words.

b. Word 1 is **wouldn't**. Spell **wouldn't**. Get ready. (Signal.) *W-O-U-L-D-N-'-T.*

c. Word 2 is **exchanging**. Spell **exchanging**. Get ready. (Signal.) *E-X-C-H-A-N-G-I-N-G.*

d. Word 3 is **requests**. Spell **requests**. Get ready. (Signal.) *R-E-Q-U-E-S-T-S.*

e. Word 4 is **stretcher**. Spell **stretcher**. Get ready. (Signal.) *S-T-R-E-T-C-H-E-R.*

f. Word 5 is **moodiness**. Spell **moodiness**. Get ready. (Signal.) *M-O-O-D-I-N-E-S-S.*

g. Word 6 is **confusing**. Spell **confusing**. Get ready. (Signal.) *C-O-N-F-U-S-I-N-G.*

h. (Give individual turns on: **1. wouldn't, 2. exchanging, 3. requests, 4. stretcher, 5. moodiness, 6. confusing.**)

LESSON 72

EXERCISE 1

Sentence

a. (Write on the board:)

> **One athlete finished the contest before everyone else.**

- I'll read the sentence on the board: **One athlete finished the contest before everyone else.**
- Let's spell some of those words.
b. Spell **athlete.** Get ready. (Signal.)
   A-T-H-L-E-T-E.
- Spell **finished.** Get ready. (Signal.)
  F-I-N-I-S-H-E-D.
- Spell **contest.** Get ready. (Signal.)
  C-O-N-T-E-S-T.
- Spell **before.** Get ready. (Signal.)
  B-E-F-O-R-E.
- Spell **everyone.** Get ready. (Signal.)
  E-V-E-R-Y-O-N-E.

EXERCISE 2

Sentence Variations

a. Get ready to write on lined paper.
- You are going to write a sentence made up of words you know how to spell. Put the right end mark at the end of the sentence.
b. The sentence is: **We excitedly exchanged great friendship.**
- Say that sentence. Get ready. (Signal.) *We excitedly exchanged great friendship.*
- (Repeat step *b* until firm.)
c. Write it. ✔
d. Get ready to check your spelling. Put an **X** next to any word you missed.
e. Spell **We.** Get ready. (Signal.) *W-E.*
- Check it. ✔
f. Spell **excitedly.** Get ready. (Signal.)
   E-X-C-I-T-E-D-L-Y.
- Check it. ✔
- (Repeat step *f* for: **exchanged, great, friendship.**)
g. What end mark did you put at the end of the sentence? (Signal.) *A period.*
- Check it. ✔
h. Fix any words you missed.

EXERCISE 3

Spelling Review

a. Get ready to spell and write some words.
b. Word 1 is **flowers.**
- What word? (Signal.) *Flowers.*
- Spell **flowers.** Get ready. (Signal.)
  F-L-O-W-E-R-S.
- Write it. ✔
c. Word 2 is **heaviest.**
- What word? (Signal.) *Heaviest.*
- Spell **heaviest.** Get ready. (Signal.)
  H-E-A-V-I-E-S-T.
- Write it. ✔
d. (Repeat step *c* for: **3. clapping, 4. investment.**)
e. I'll spell each word.
- Put an **X** next to any word you missed and write that word correctly.
- (Spell each word twice. Write the words on the board as you spell them.)

1. flowers	**3. clapping**
2. heaviest	**4. investment**

EXERCISE 1

Sentence

a. (Write on the board:)

> **One athlete finished the contest before everyone else.**

- I'll read the sentence on the board: **One athlete finished the contest before everyone else.**
- Let's spell some of those words.
b. Spell **athlete.** Get ready. (Signal.)
A-T-H-L-E-T-E.
- Spell **finished.** Get ready. (Signal.)
F-I-N-I-S-H-E-D.
- Spell **contest.** Get ready. (Signal.)
C-O-N-T-E-S-T.
- Spell **before.** Get ready. (Signal.)
B-E-F-O-R-E.
- Spell **everyone.** Get ready. (Signal.)
E-V-E-R-Y-O-N-E.

EXERCISE 2

Morphographic Analysis

a. (Write on the board:)

1. unfounded = _____

2. requesting = _____

3. signal = _____

4. extract = _____

5. funny = _____

6. tensest = _____

- Number your paper from 1 to 6. ✔
- Write the morphographs that go in each blank. Put plus signs between the morphographs. ✔

b. (Write to show:)

1. **unfounded** = **un + found + ed**

2. **requesting** = **re + quest + ing**

3. **signal** = **sign + al**

4. **extract** = **ex + tract**

5. **funny** = **fun + y**

6. **tensest** = **tense + est**

c. Check your work. Make an **X** next to any item you got wrong. ✔

EXERCISE 3

Prompted Review

a. (Write on the board:)

1. unintended
2. delightful
3. contended
4. quizzing
5. you'll
6. rainiest

b. Word 1 is **unintended.** Spell **unintended.** Get ready. (Signal.) *U-N-I-N-T-E-N-D-E-D.*
c. Word 2 is **delightful.** Spell **delightful.** Get ready. (Signal.) *D-E-L-I-G-H-T-F-U-L.*
d. (Repeat step c for: **3. contended, 4. quizzing, 5. you'll, 6. rainiest.**)
e. (Erase the board.)
- Now spell those words without looking.
f. Word 1 is **unintended.** Spell **unintended.** Get ready. (Signal.) *U-N-I-N-T-E-N-D-E-D.*
g. Word 2 is **delightful.** Spell **delightful.** Get ready. (Signal.) *D-E-L-I-G-H-T-F-U-L.*
h. (Repeat step g for: **3. contended, 4. quizzing, 5. you'll, 6. rainiest.**)
i. (Give individual turns on: **1. unintended, 2. delightful, 3. contended, 4. quizzing, 5. you'll, 6. rainiest.**)

EXERCISE 1

Sentence

a. You're going to write this sentence: **One athlete finished the contest before everyone else.**

b. Say the sentence. Get ready. (Signal.) *One athlete finished the contest before everyone else.*

c. Write the sentence. ✔

d. (Write on the board:)

> **One athlete finished the contest before everyone else.**

e. Check your work. Make an **X** next to any word you got wrong. ✔

EXERCISE 2

Word Building

a. (Write on the board:)

> 1. pre + tend + ing =
> 2. drain + age =
> 3. study + es =
> 4. star + ing =
> 5. con + tract + ing =
> 6. ex + cite + ing =

b. You're going to write the words that go after the equal signs.

• Some of these words follow the final **e** rule. Some follow the doubling rule or the **y-to-i** rule. Be careful.

• Number your paper from 1 to 6. ✔

c. Word 1: Write **pretending** on your paper. ✔

d. Do the rest of the words on your own. ✔

e. Check your work. Make an **X** next to any word you got wrong.

f. Word 1. Spell **pretending.** Get ready. (Tap for each letter.) *P-R-E-T-E-N-D-I-N-G.*

• (Repeat for: **2. drainage, 3. studies, 4. starring, 5. contracting, 6. exciting.**)

EXERCISE 3

Spelling Review

a. You're going to spell words.

b. Word 1 is **strengthening.** Spell **strengthening.** Get ready. (Signal.) *S-T-R-E-N-G-T-H-E-N-I-N-G.*

c. Word 2 is **invaluable.** Spell **invaluable.** Get ready. (Signal.) *I-N-V-A-L-U-A-B-L-E.*

d. Word 3 is **marries.** Spell **marries.** Get ready. (Signal.) *M-A-R-R-I-E-S.*

e. Word 4 is **sleeplessness.** Spell **sleeplessness.** Get ready. (Signal.) *S-L-E-E-P-L-E-S-S-N-E-S-S.*

f. Word 5 is **intense.** Spell **intense.** Get ready. (Signal.) *I-N-T-E-N-S-E.*

g. Word 6 is **unplanned.** Spell **unplanned.** Get ready. (Signal.) *U-N-P-L-A-N-N-E-D.*

h. (Give individual turns on: **1. strengthening, 2. invaluable, 3. marries, 4. sleeplessness, 5. intense, 6. unplanned.**)

EXERCISE 1

Word Introduction

a. (Write on the board:)

> danger
> beauty
> cover
> sudden

b. Get ready to read these words.
- First word: **danger.** What word? (Signal.) *Danger.*
c. Next word: **beauty.** What word? (Signal.) *Beauty.*
- (Repeat for: **cover, sudden.**)
d. Now spell those words.
- Spell **danger.** Get ready. (Signal.) *D-A-N-G-E-R.*
e. Spell **beauty.** Get ready. (Signal.) *B-E-A-U-T-Y.*
- (Repeat for: **cover, sudden.**)
f. (Erase the board.)
- Spell the words without looking.
g. Spell **danger.** Get ready. (Signal.) *D-A-N-G-E-R.*
h. Spell **beauty.** Get ready. (Signal.) *B-E-A-U-T-Y.*
- (Repeat for: **cover, sudden.**)

EXERCISE 2

Sentence Variations

a. Get ready to write on lined paper.
- You are going to write a sentence made up of words you know how to spell. Put the right end mark at the end of the sentence.
b. The sentence is: **Was the athlete friendly and thoughtful?**
- Say that sentence. Get ready. (Signal.) *Was the athlete friendly and thoughtful?*
- (Repeat step *b* until firm.)
c. Write it. ✔
d. Get ready to check your spelling. Put an **X** next to any word you missed.
e. Spell **Was.** Get ready. (Signal.) *W-A-S.*
- Check it. ✔

f. Spell **the.** Get ready. (Signal.) *T-H-E.*
- Check it. ✔
- (Repeat step *f* for: **athlete, friendly, and, thoughtful.**)
g. What end mark did you put at the end of the sentence? (Signal.) *A question mark.*
- Check it. ✔
h. Fix any words you missed.

EXERCISE 3

Spelling Review

a. Get ready to spell and write some words.
b. Word 1 is **requested.**
- What word? (Signal.) *Requested.*
- Spell **requested.** Get ready. (Signal.) *R-E-Q-U-E-S-T-E-D.*
- Write it. ✔
c. Word 2 is **speediest.**
- What word? (Signal.) *Speediest.*
- Spell **speediest.** Get ready. (Signal.) *S-P-E-E-D-I-E-S-T.*
- Write it. ✔
d. (Repeat step *c* for: **3. unsnapped, 4. mismatched.**)
e. I'll spell each word.
- Put an **X** next to any word you missed and write that word correctly.
- (Spell each word twice. Write the words on the board as you spell them.)

> 1. requested   3. unsnapped
> 2. speediest   4. mismatched

EXERCISE 1

Word Introduction

> **Note:** Pronounce the sound /ē/ like the letter name **E**.

a. (Write on the board:)

> chief
> niece
> grief
> brief
> thief

b. Get ready to read these words.
- In each of these words, the sound /ē/ is spelled **i-e**.
- First word: **chief**. What word? (Signal.) *Chief.*
c. Next word: **niece**. What word? (Signal.) *Niece.*
- (Repeat for: **grief, brief, thief.**)
d. Now spell those words.
- Spell **chief**. Get ready. (Signal.) *C-H-I-E-F.*
e. Spell **niece**. Get ready. (Signal.) *N-I-E-C-E.*
- (Repeat for: **grief, brief, thief.**)
f. (Erase the board.)
- Spell the words without looking.
g. Spell **chief**. Get ready. (Signal.) *C-H-I-E-F.*
h. Spell **niece**. Get ready. (Signal.) *N-I-E-C-E.*
- (Repeat for: **grief, brief, thief.**)

EXERCISE 2

Word Building

a. (Write on the board:)

> 1. re + cover + ing =
> 2. re + cite + al =
> 3. slug + ish + ly =
> 4. waste + ful + ness =
> 5. dis + tract + ed =
> 6. mis + quote + ing =

b. You're going to write the words that go after the equal signs.
- Some of these words follow the final **e** rule. Be careful.
- Number your paper from 1 to 6. ✔

c. Word 1: Write **recovering** on your paper. ✔
d. Do the rest of the words on your own. ✔
e. Check your work. Make an **X** next to any word you got wrong.
f. Word 1. Spell **recovering**. Get ready. (Tap for each letter.) *R-E-C-O-V-E-R-I-N-G.*
- (Repeat for: **2. recital, 3. sluggishly, 4. wastefulness, 5. distracted, 6. misquoting.**)

EXERCISE 3

Prompted Review

a. (Write on the board:)

> 1. athlete
> 2. danger
> 3. studies
> 4. tensely
> 5. suddenly
> 6. recovering

b. Word 1 is **athlete**. Spell **athlete**. Get ready. (Signal.) *A-T-H-L-E-T-E.*
c. Word 2 is **danger**. Spell **danger**. Get ready. (Signal.) *D-A-N-G-E-R.*
d. (Repeat step c for: **3. studies, 4. tensely, 5. suddenly, 6. recovering.**)
e. (Erase the board.)
- Now spell those words without looking.
f. Word 1 is athlete. Spell **athlete**. Get ready. (Signal.) *A-T-H-L-E-T-E.*
g. Word 2 is danger. Spell **danger**. Get ready. (Signal.) *D-A-N-G-E-R.*
h. (Repeat step g for: **3. studies, 4. tensely, 5. suddenly, 6. recovering.**)
i. (Give individual turns on: **1. athlete, 2. danger, 3. studies, 4. tensely, 5. suddenly, 6. recovering.**)

EXERCISE 1
Word Introduction
a. (Write on the board:)

> grief
> chief
> thief
> niece
> brief

b. In each of these words, the sound /ē/ is spelled **i-e**.
- Spell **grief**. Get ready. (Signal.) *G-R-I-E-F.*
c. Spell **chief**. Get ready. (Signal.) *C-H-I-E-F.*
- (Repeat for: **thief, niece, brief.**)
d (Erase the board.)
- Spell the words without looking.
e. Spell **grief**. Get ready. (Signal.) *G-R-I-E-F.*
f. Spell **chief**. Get ready. (Signal.) *C-H-I-E-F.*
- (Repeat for: **thief, niece, brief.**)

EXERCISE 2
Morphographic Analysis
a. (Write on the board:)

> 1. **exporting** = _____
>
> 2. **confused** = _____
>
> 3. **lengthening** = _____
>
> 4. **maddening** = _____
>
> 5. **luckily** = _____
>
> 6. **starring** = _____

- Number your paper from 1 to 6. ✔
- Write the morphographs that go in each blank. Put plus signs between the morphographs. ✔

b. (Write to show:)

> 1. **exporting** = ex + port + ing
>
> 2. **confused** = con + fuse + ed
>
> 3. **lengthening** = length + en + ing
>
> 4. **maddening** = mad + en + ing
>
> 5. **luckily** = luck + y + ly
>
> 6. **starring** = star + ing

c. Check your work. Make an **X** next to any item you got wrong. ✔

EXERCISE 3
Spelling Review
a. You're going to spell words.
b. Word 1 is **everyone**. Spell **everyone**. Get ready. (Signal.) *E-V-E-R-Y-O-N-E.*
c. Word 2 is **beauty**. Spell **beauty**. Get ready. (Signal.) *B-E-A-U-T-Y.*
d. Word 3 is **reciting**. Spell **reciting**. Get ready. (Signal.) *R-E-C-I-T-I-N-G.*
e. Word 4 is **investment**. Spell **investment**. Get ready. (Signal.) *I-N-V-E-S-T-M-E-N-T.*
f. Word 5 is **business**. Spell **business**. Get ready. (Signal.) *B-U-S-I-N-E-S-S.*
g. Word 6 is **previewed**. Spell **previewed**. Get ready. (Signal.) *P-R-E-V-I-E-W-E-D.*
h. (Give individual turns on: **1. everyone, 2. beauty, 3. reciting, 4. investment, 5. business, 6. previewed.**)

EXERCISE 1

Sentence Variations

a. Get ready to write on lined paper.

• You are going to write a sentence made up of words you know how to spell. Put the right end mark at the end of the sentence.

b. The sentence is: **Business couldn't be more exciting.**

• Say that sentence. Get ready. (Signal.) *Business couldn't be more exciting.*

• (Repeat step *b* until firm.)

c. Write it. ✔

d. Get ready to check your spelling. Put an **X** next to any word you missed.

e. Spell **Business**. Get ready. (Signal.) *B-U-S-I-N-E-S-S.*

• Check it. ✔

f. Spell **couldn't**. Get ready. (Signal.) *C-O-U-L-D-N-'-T.*

• Check it. ✔

• (Repeat step *f* for: **be, more, exciting.**)

g. What end mark did you put at the end of the sentence? (Signal.) *A period.*

• Check it. ✔

h. Fix any words you missed.

EXERCISE 2

Word Building

a. (Write on the board:)

> 1. athlete + ic =
> 2. beauty + ful =
> 3. brief + ly =
> 4. sudden + ness =
> 5. fine + ish + ing =
> 6. re + sent + ment =

b. You're going to write the words that go after the equal signs.

• Some of these words follow the final **e** rule. Some follow the **y-to-i** rule. Be careful.

• Number your paper from 1 to 6. ✔

c. Word 1: Write **athletic** on your paper. ✔

d. Do the rest of the words on your own. ✔

e. Check your work. Make an **X** next to any word you got wrong.

f. Word 1. Spell **athletic**. Get ready. (Tap for each letter.) *A-T-H-L-E-T-I-C.*

• (Repeat for: **2. beautiful, 3. briefly, 4. suddenness, 5. finishing, 6. resentment.**)

EXERCISE 3

Spelling Review

a. You're going to spell words.

b. Word 1 is **thief**. Spell **thief**. Get ready. (Signal.) *T-H-I-E-F.*

c. Word 2 is **before**. Spell **before**. Get ready. (Signal.) *B-E-F-O-R-E.*

d. Word 3 is **recover**. Spell **recover**. Get ready. (Signal.) *R-E-C-O-V-E-R.*

e. Word 4 is **quickly**. Spell **quickly**. Get ready. (Signal.) *Q-U-I-C-K-L-Y.*

f. Word 5 is **contract**. Spell **contract**. Get ready. (Signal.) *C-O-N-T-R-A-C-T.*

g. Word 6 is **hurries**. Spell **hurries**. Get ready. (Signal.) *H-U-R-R-I-E-S.*

h. (Give individual turns on: **1. thief, 2. before, 3. recover, 4. quickly, 5. contract, 6. hurries.**)

EXERCISE 1

Word Introduction

a. (Write on the board:)

> reason
> type
> house
> first

b. Get ready to read these words.
- First word: **reason.** What word? (Signal.) *Reason.*
c. Next word: **type.** What word? (Signal.) *Type.*
- (Repeat for: **house, first.**)
d. Now spell those words.
- Spell **reason.** Get ready. (Signal.) *R-E-A-S-O-N.*
e. Spell **type.** Get ready. (Signal.) *T-Y-P-E.*
- (Repeat for: **house, first.**)
f. (Erase the board.)
- Spell the words without looking.
g. Spell **reason.** Get ready. (Signal.) *R-E-A-S-O-N.*
h. Spell **type.** Get ready. (Signal.) *T-Y-P-E.*
- (Repeat for: **house, first.**)

EXERCISE 2

Morphographic Analysis

a. (Write on the board:)

> 1. chiefly = _____
>
> 2. contended = _____
>
> 3. explain = _____
>
> 4. government = _____
>
> 5. pretended = _____
>
> 6. breathing = _____

- Number your paper from 1 to 6. ✔
- Write the morphographs that go in each blank. Put plus signs between the morphographs. ✔

b. (Write to show:)

> 1. chiefly = chief + ly
>
> 2. contended = con + tend + ed
>
> 3. explain = ex + plain
>
> 4. government = govern + ment
>
> 5. pretended = pre + tend + ed
>
> 6. breathing = breathe + ing

c. Check your work. Make an **X** next to any item you got wrong. ✔

EXERCISE 3

Spelling Review

a. Get ready to spell and write some words.
b. Word 1 is **joyfully.**
- What word? (Signal.) *Joyfully.*
- Spell **joyfully.** Get ready. (Signal.) *J-O-Y-F-U-L-L-Y.*
- Write it. ✔
c. Word 2 is **defacing.**
- What word? (Signal.) *Defacing.*
- Spell **defacing.** Get ready. (Signal.) *D-E-F-A-C-I-N-G.*
- Write it. ✔
d. (Repeat step c for: **3. denial, 4. unfriendliness.**)
e. I'll spell each word.
- Put an **X** next to any word you missed and write that word correctly.
- (Spell each word twice. Write the words on the board as you spell them.)

> 1. joyfully   3. denial
> 2. defacing   4. unfriendliness

LESSON 80

EXERCISE 1

Test

a. Today you have a spelling test. Number your lined paper from 1 through 10. ✔

b. Word 1 is **chief.** What word? (Signal.) *Chief.*

• Write the word **chief.** ✔

c. Word 2 is **beautiful.** What word? (Signal.) *Beautiful.*

• Write the word **beautiful.** ✔

d. (Repeat step c for: **3. athlete, 4. worries, 5. shopped, 6. lucky, 7. detract, 8. quest, 9. breathe, 10. children.**)

e. Pick up your red pen. ✔
Make an **X** next to any word you spelled wrong.

• (Write on the board:)

1. chief	6. lucky
2. beautiful	7. detract
3. athlete	8. quest
4. worries	9. breathe
5. shopped	10. children

• Write the correct spelling next to any word you spelled wrong.
(Observe students and give feedback.)

EXERCISE 1

Affix Introduction

a. (Write on the board:)

> **1. pro + long =**
> **2. pro + claim =**
> **3. pro + file =**

- All these words have the morphograph **pro.**

b. Number your paper from 1 to 3. ✔

c. Add the morphographs together to make new words. Write just the new words. ✔

d. Check your work. Make an **X** next to any word you got wrong.

e. Word 1. Spell **prolong.** Get ready. (Tap for each letter.) *P-R-O-L-O-N-G.*

- (Repeat for: **2. proclaim, 3. profile.**)

EXERCISE 2

Word Building

a. (Write on the board:)

> **1. beauty + ful + ly =**
> **2. in + cite + ed =**
> **3. quick + en + ing =**
> **4. study + ing =**
> **5. pre + plan + ed =**
> **6. sturdy + ness =**

b. You're going to write the words that go after the equal signs.

- Some of these words follow the final **e** rule. Some follow the doubling rule or the **y-to-i rule**. Be careful.

- Number your paper from 1 to 6. ✔

c. Word 1: Write **beautifully** on your paper. ✔

d. Do the rest of the words on your own. ✔

e. Check your work. Make an **X** next to any word you got wrong.

f. Word 1. Spell **beautifully.** Get ready. (Tap for each letter.) *B-E-A-U-T-I-F-U-L-L-Y.*

- (Repeat for: **2. incited, 3. quickening, 4. studying, 5. preplanned, 6. sturdiness.**)

EXERCISE 3

Spelling Review

a. You're going to spell words.

b. Word 1 is **athlete.** Spell **athlete.** Get ready. (Signal.) *A-T-H-L-E-T-E.*

c. Word 2 is **danger.** Spell **danger.** Get ready. (Signal.) *D-A-N-G-E-R.*

d. Word 3 is **heavier.** Spell **heavier.** Get ready. (Signal.) *H-E-A-V-I-E-R.*

e. Word 4 is **quizzed.** Spell **quizzed.** Get ready. (Signal.) *Q-U-I-Z-Z-E-D.*

f. Word 5 is **sturdiest.** Spell **sturdiest.** Get ready. (Signal.) *S-T-U-R-D-I-E-S-T.*

g. Word 6 is **reason.** Spell **reason.** Get ready. (Signal.) *R-E-A-S-O-N.*

h. (Give individual turns on: **1. athlete, 2. danger, 3. heavier, 4. quizzed, 5. sturdiest, 6. reason.**)

EXERCISE 1

Affix Introduction

a. (Write on the board:)

> 1. act + ive =
> 2. pass + ive =
> 3. create + ive =

- All these words have the morphograph **i-v-e.**
b. Number your paper from 1 to 3. ✔
c. Add the morphographs together to make new words. Write just the new words. ✔
d. Check your work. Make an **X** next to any word you got wrong.
e. Word 1. Spell **active.** Get ready. (Tap for each letter.) *A-C-T-I-V-E.*
- (Repeat for: **2. passive, 3. creative.**)

EXERCISE 2

Morphographic Analysis

a. (Write on the board:)

> 1. proclaimed = _____
>
> 2. profound = _____
>
> 3. mistaken = _____
>
> 4. intensely = _____
>
> 5. expressive = _____
>
> 6. describing = _____

- Number your paper from 1 to 6. ✔
- Write the morphographs that go in each blank. Put plus signs between the morphographs. ✔

b. (Write to show:)

> 1. **proclaimed = pro + claim + ed**
>
> 2. **profound = pro + found**
>
> 3. **mistaken = mis + take + en**
>
> 4. **intensely = in + tense + ly**
>
> 5. **expressive = ex + press + ive**
>
> 6. **describing = de + scribe + ing**

c. Check your work. Make an **X** next to any item you got wrong. ✔

EXERCISE 3

Prompted Review

a. (Write on the board:)

> 1. **reasonable**
> 2. **chiefly**
> 3. **everyone**
> 4. **nastiest**
> 5. **untyped**
> 6. **misspelled**

b. Word 1 is **reasonable.** Spell **reasonable.** Get ready. (Signal.) *R-E-A-S-O-N-A-B-L-E.*
c. Word 2 is **chiefly.** Spell **chiefly.** Get ready. (Signal.) *C-H-I-E-F-L-Y.*
d. (Repeat step c for: **3. everyone, 4. nastiest, 5. untyped, 6. misspelled.**)
e. (Erase the board.)
- Now spell those words without looking.
f. Word 1 is **reasonable.** Spell **reasonable.** Get ready. (Signal.) *R-E-A-S-O-N-A-B-L-E.*
g. Word 2 is **chiefly.** Spell **chiefly.** Get ready. (Signal.) *C-H-I-E-F-L-Y.*
h. (Repeat step g for: **3. everyone, 4. nastiest, 5. untyped, 6. misspelled.**)
i. (Give individual turns on: **1. reasonable, 2. chiefly, 3. everyone, 4. nastiest, 5. untyped, 6. misspelled.**)

LESSON 83

EXERCISE 1

Sentence

a. (Write on the board:)

> **Our second surprise was especially exciting.**

- I'll read the sentence on the board: **Our second surprise was especially exciting.**
- Let's spell some of those words.

b. Spell **Our.** Get ready. (Signal.) *O-U-R.*
- Spell **second.** Get ready. (Signal.) *S-E-C-O-N-D.*
- Spell **surprise.** Get ready. (Signal.) *S-U-R-P-R-I-S-E.*
- Spell **especially.** Get ready. (Signal.) *E-S-P-E-C-I-A-L-L-Y.*
- Spell **exciting.** Get ready. (Signal.) *E-X-C-I-T-I-N-G.*

c. Copy this sentence on lined paper. (Observe students and give feedback.)

d. Read the sentence you just copied. Get ready. (Signal.) *Our second surprise was especially exciting.*

EXERCISE 2

Word Building

a. (Write on the board:)

> 1. create + ive =
> 2. pro + file + ing =
> 3. mis + shape + en + ed =
> 4. con + fuse + ing =
> 5. re + fuse + al =
> 6. sign + al + ing =

b. You're going to write the words that go after the equal signs.
- Some of these words follow the final **e** rule. Be careful.
- Number your paper from 1 to 6. ✔

c. Word 1: Write **creative** on your paper. ✔

d. Do the rest of the words on your own. ✔

e. Check your work. Make an **X** next to any word you got wrong.

f. Word 1. Spell **creative.** Get ready. (Tap for each letter.) *C-R-E-A-T-I-V-E.*
- (Repeat for: **2. profiling, 3. misshapened, 4. confusing, 5. refusal, 6. signaling.**)

EXERCISE 3

Spelling Review

a. You're going to spell words.

b. Word 1 is **expressive.** Spell **expressive.** Get ready. (Signal.) *E-X-P-R-E-S-S-I-V-E.*

c. Word 2 is **proclaiming.** Spell **proclaiming.** Get ready. (Signal.) *P-R-O-C-L-A-I-M-I-N-G.*

d. Word 3 is **carries.** Spell **carries.** Get ready. (Signal.) *C-A-R-R-I-E-S.*

e. Word 4 is **suddenness.** Spell **suddenness.** Get ready. (Signal.) *S-U-D-D-E-N-N-E-S-S.*

f. Word 5 is **distracted.** Spell **distracted.** Get ready. (Signal.) *D-I-S-T-R-A-C-T-E-D.*

g. Word 6 is **tensely.** Spell **tensely.** Get ready. (Signal.) *T-E-N-S-E-L-Y.*

h. (Give individual turns on: **1. expressive, 2. proclaiming, 3. carries, 4. suddenness, 5. distracted, 6. tensely.**)

LESSON 84

EXERCISE 1

Sentence

a. (Write on the board:)

> **Our second surprise was especially exciting.**

- I'll read the sentence on the board: **Our second surprise was especially exciting.**
- Let's spell some of those words.

b. Spell **Our.** Get ready. (Signal.) *O-U-R.*

- Spell **second.** Get ready. (Signal.) *S-E-C-O-N-D.*
- Spell **surprise.** Get ready. (Signal.) *S-U-R-P-R-I-S-E.*
- Spell **especially.** Get ready. (Signal.) *E-S-P-E-C-I-A-L-L-Y.*
- Spell **exciting.** Get ready. (Signal.) *E-X-C-I-T-I-N-G.*

c. (Erase the board.)

d. Now let's spell some of the words in that sentence without looking.

- Spell **Our.** Get ready. (Signal.) *O-U-R.*
- Spell **second.** Get ready. (Signal.) *S-E-C-O-N-D.*
- Spell **surprise.** Get ready. (Signal.) *S-U-R-P-R-I-S-E.*
- Spell **especially.** Get ready. (Signal.) *E-S-P-E-C-I-A-L-L-Y.*
- Spell **exciting.** Get ready. (Signal.) *E-X-C-I-T-I-N-G.*

EXERCISE 2

Sentence Variations

a. Get ready to write on lined paper.

- You are going to write a sentence made up of words you know how to spell. Put the right end mark at the end of the sentence.

b. The sentence is: **The athletic chief acted quickly and forcefully.**

- Say that sentence. Get ready. (Signal.) *The athletic chief acted quickly and forcefully.*
- (Repeat step *b* until firm.)

c. Write it. ✔

d. Get ready to check your spelling. Put an **X** next to any word you missed.

e. Spell **The.** Get ready. (Signal.) *T-H-E.*

- Check it. ✔

f. Spell **athletic.** Get ready. (Signal.) *A-T-H-L-E-T-I-C.*

- Check it. ✔
- (Repeat step *f* for: **chief, acted, quickly, and, forcefully.**)

g. What end mark did you put at the end of the sentence? (Signal.) *A period.*

- Check it. ✔

h. Fix any words you missed.

EXERCISE 3

Spelling Review

a. You're going to spell words.

b. Word 1 is **blackness.** Spell **blackness.** Get ready. (Signal.) *B-L-A-C-K-N-E-S-S.*

c. Word 2 is **cities.** Spell **cities.** Get ready. (Signal.) *C-I-T-I-E-S.*

d. Word 3 is **hotter.** Spell **hotter.** Get ready. (Signal.) *H-O-T-T-E-R.*

e. Word 4 is **watches.** Spell **watches.** Get ready. (Signal.) *W-A-T-C-H-E-S.*

f. Word 5 is **government.** Spell **government.** Get ready. (Signal.) *G-O-V-E-R-N-M-E-N-T.*

g. Word 6 is **profile.** Spell **profile.** Get ready. (Signal.) *P-R-O-F-I-L-E.*

h. (Give individual turns on: **1. blackness, 2. cities, 3. hotter, 4. watches, 5. government, 6. profile.**)

EXERCISE 1

Sentence

a. (Write on the board:)

> **Our second surprise was especially exciting.**

- I'll read the sentence on the board: **Our second surprise was especially exciting.**
- Let's spell some of those words.

b. Spell **Our.** Get ready. (Signal.) *O-U-R.*
- Spell **second.** Get ready. (Signal.) *S-E-C-O-N-D.*
- Spell **surprise.** Get ready. (Signal.) *S-U-R-P-R-I-S-E.*
- Spell **especially.** Get ready. (Signal.) *E-S-P-E-C-I-A-L-L-Y.*
- Spell **exciting.** Get ready. (Signal.) *E-X-C-I-T-I-N-G.*

c. (Erase the board.)

d. Now let's spell some of the words in that sentence without looking.
- Spell **Our.** Get ready. (Signal.) *O-U-R.*
- Spell **second.** Get ready. (Signal.) *S-E-C-O-N-D.*
- Spell **surprise.** Get ready. (Signal.) *S-U-R-P-R-I-S-E.*
- Spell **especially.** Get ready. (Signal.) *E-S-P-E-C-I-A-L-L-Y.*
- Spell **exciting.** Get ready. (Signal.) *E-X-C-I-T-I-N-G.*

EXERCISE 2

Word Building

a. (Write on the board:)

> 1. in + act + ive =
> 2. carry + age =
> 3. quote + able =
> 4. re + move + al =
> 5. drop + er =
> 6. re + act + ive =

b. You're going to write the words that go after the equal signs.
- Some of these words follow the final **e** rule. Some follow the doubling rule or the **y-to-i** rule. Be careful.
- Number your paper from 1 to 6. ✔

c. Word 1: Write **inactive** on your paper. ✔

d. Do the rest of the words on your own. ✔

e. Check your work. Make an **X** next to any word you got wrong.

f. Word 1. Spell **inactive.** Get ready. (Tap for each letter.) *I-N-A-C-T-I-V-E.*
- (Repeat for: **2. carriage, 3. quotable, 4. removal, 5. dropper, 6. reactive.**)

EXERCISE 3

Spelling Review

a. You're going to spell words.

b. Word 1 is **confusing.** Spell **confusing.** Get ready. (Signal.) *C-O-N-F-U-S-I-N-G.*

c. Word 2 is **expressive.** Spell **expressive.** Get ready. (Signal.) *E-X-P-R-E-S-S-I-V-E.*

d. Word 3 is **proclaim.** Spell **proclaim.** Get ready. (Signal.) *P-R-O-C-L-A-I-M.*

e. Word 4 is **copies.** Spell **copies.** Get ready. (Signal.) *C-O-P-I-E-S.*

f. Word 5 is **pretending.** Spell **pretending.** Get ready. (Signal.) *P-R-E-T-E-N-D-I-N-G.*

g. Word 6 is **roominess.** Spell **roominess.** Get ready. (Signal.) *R-O-O-M-I-N-E-S-S.*

h. (Give individual turns on: **1. confusing, 2. expressive, 3. proclaim, 4. copies, 5. pretending, 6. roominess.**)

EXERCISE 1

Sentence

a. You're going to write this sentence: **Our second surprise was especially exciting.**

b. Say the sentence. Get ready. (Signal.) *Our second surprise was especially exciting.*

c. Write the sentence. ✔

d. (Write on the board:)

> **Our second surprise was especially exciting.**

e. Check your work. Make an **X** next to any word you got wrong. ✔

EXERCISE 2

Sentence Variations

a. Get ready to write on lined paper.

• You are going to write a sentence made up of words you know how to spell. Put the right end mark at the end of the sentence.

b. The sentence is: **You breathe hard while recovering from an intense race.**

• Say that sentence. Get ready. (Signal.) *You breathe hard while recovering from an intense race.*

• (Repeat step *b* until firm.)

c. Write it on the line. ✔

d. Get ready to check your spelling. Put an **X** next to any word you missed.

e. Spell **You.** Get ready. (Signal.) *Y-O-U.*

• Check it. ✔

f. Spell **breathe.** Get ready. (Signal.) *B-R-E-A-T-H-E.*

• Check it. ✔

• (Repeat step *f* for: **hard, while, recovering, from, an, intense, race.**)

g. What end mark did you put at the end of the sentence? (Signal.) *A period.*

• Check it. ✔

h. Fix any words you missed.

EXERCISE 3

Spelling Review

a. You're going to spell words.

b. Word 1 is **removing.** Spell **removing.** Get ready. (Signal.) *R-E-M-O-V-I-N-G.*

c. Word 2 is **poisoning.** Spell **poisoning.** Get ready. (Signal.) *P-O-I-S-O-N-I-N-G.*

d. Word 3 is **strangely.** Spell **strangely.** Get ready. (Signal.) *S-T-R-A-N-G-E-L-Y.*

e. Word 4 is **depressed.** Spell **depressed.** Get ready. (Signal.) *D-E-P-R-E-S-S-E-D.*

f. Word 5 is **maddening.** Spell **maddening.** Get ready. (Signal.) *M-A-D-D-E-N-I-N-G.*

g. Word 6 is **earliest.** Spell **earliest.** Get ready. (Signal.) *E-A-R-L-I-E-S-T.*

h. (Give individual turns on: **1. removing, 2. poisoning, 3. strangely, 4. depressed, 5. maddening, 6. earliest.**)

EXERCISE 1

Affix Introduction

a. (Write on the board:)

> 1. act + ion =
> 2. state + ion =
> 3. quest + ion =

- All these words have the morphograph **i-o-n.**
b. Number your paper from 1 to 3. ✔
c. Add the morphographs together to make new words. ✔
d. Check your work. Make an **X** next to any word you got wrong.
e. Word 1. Spell **action.** Get ready. (Tap for each letter.) *A-C-T-I-O-N.*
- (Repeat for: **2. station, 3. question.**)

EXERCISE 2

Sentence Variations

a. Get ready to write on lined paper.
- You are going to write a sentence made up of words you know how to spell. Put the right end mark at the end of the sentence.
b. The sentence is: **The children carried some boxes earlier.**
- Say that sentence. Get ready. (Signal.) *The children carried some boxes earlier.*
- (Repeat step *b* until firm.)
c. Write it. ✔
d. Get ready to check your spelling. Put an **X** next to any word you missed.
e. Spell **The.** Get ready. (Signal.) *T-H-E.*
- Check it. ✔
f. Spell **children.** Get ready. (Signal.) *C-H-I-L-D-R-E-N.*
- Check it. ✔
- (Repeat step *f* for: **carried, some, boxes, earlier.**)
g. What end mark did you put at the end of the sentence? (Signal.) *A period.*
- Check it. ✔
h. Fix any words you missed.

EXERCISE 3

Prompted Review

a. (Write on the board:)

> 1. excited
> 2. creative
> 3. especially
> 4. danger
> 5. pretended
> 6. proclaimed

b. Word 1 is **excited.** Spell **excited.** Get ready. (Signal.) *E-X-C-I-T-E-D.*
c. Word 2 is **creative.** Spell **creative.** Get ready. (Signal.) *C-R-E-A-T-I-V-E.*
d. (Repeat for: **3. especially, 4. danger, 5. pretended, 6. proclaimed.**)
e (Erase the board.)
- Now spell those words without looking.
f. Word 1 is **excited.** Spell **excited.** Get ready. (Signal.) *E-X-C-I-T-E-D.*
g. Word 2 is **creative.** Spell **creative.** Get ready. (Signal.) *C-R-E-A-T-I-V-E.*
h. (Repeat for: **3. especially, 4. danger, 5. pretended, 6. proclaimed.**)
i. (Give individual turns on: **1. excited, 2. creative, 3. especially, 4. danger, 5. pretended, 6. proclaimed.**)

LESSON 88

EXERCISE 1

Morphographic Analysis

a. (Write on the board:)

> 1. passion = _____
>
> 2. notion = _____
>
> 3. childishly = _____
>
> 4. friendliness = _____
>
> 5. harmlessness = _____
>
> 6. carriage = _____

- Number your paper from 1 to 6. ✔
- Write the morphographs that go in each blank. Put plus signs between the morphographs. ✔

b. (Write to show:)

> 1. passion = pass + ion
>
> 2. notion = note + ion
>
> 3. childishly = child + ish + ly
>
> 4. friendliness = friend + ly + ness
>
> 5. harmlessness = harm + less + ness
>
> 6. carriage = carry + age

c. Check your work. Make an **X** next to any item you got wrong. ✔

EXERCISE 2

Sentence Variations

a. Get ready to write on lined paper.
- You are going to write a sentence made up of words you know how to spell. Put the right end mark at the end of the sentence.

b. The sentence is: **Someone reserved a sunny spot for swimming.**
- Say that sentence. Get ready. (Signal.) *Someone reserved a sunny spot for swimming.*
- (Repeat step *b* until firm.)

c. Write it. ✔
d. Get ready to check your spelling. Put an **X** next to any word you missed.
e. Spell **Someone.** Get ready. (Signal.) *S-O-M-E-O-N-E.*
- Check it. ✔
f. Spell **reserved.** Get ready. (Signal.) *R-E-S-E-R-V-E-D.*
- Check it. ✔
- (Repeat step *f* for: **a, sunny, spot, for, swimming.**)
g. What end mark did you put at the end of the sentence? (Signal.) *A period.*
- Check it. ✔
h. Fix any words you missed.

EXERCISE 3

Spelling Review

a. You're going to spell words.
b. Word 1 is **furry.** Spell **furry.** Get ready. (Signal.) *F-U-R-R-Y.*
c. Word 2 is **second.** Spell **second.** Get ready. (Signal.) *S-E-C-O-N-D.*
d. Word 3 is **quotable.** Spell **quotable.** Get ready. (Signal.) *Q-U-O-T-A-B-L-E.*
e. Word 4 is **requested.** Spell **requested.** Get ready. (Signal.) *R-E-Q-U-E-S-T-E-D.*
f. Word 5 is **athlete.** Spell **athlete.** Get ready. (Signal.) *A-T-H-L-E-T-E.*
g. Word 6 is **chiefly.** Spell **chiefly.** Get ready. (Signal.) *C-H-I-E-F-L-Y.*
h. (Give individual turns on: **1. furry, 2. second, 3. quotable, 4. requested, 5. athlete, 6. chiefly.**)

EXERCISE 1

Word Building

a. (Write on the board:)

> 1. act + ive + ly =
> 2. re + late + ion =
> 3. tense + ion =
> 4. ex + press + ive =
> 5. in + act + ive =
> 6. marry + age =

b. You're going to write the words that go after the equal signs.
- Some of these words follow the final **e** rule. Some follow the **y-to-i** rule. Be careful.
- Number your paper from 1 to 6. ✔
c. Word 1: Write **actively** on your paper. ✔
d. Do the rest of the words on your own. ✔
e. Check your work. Make an **X** next to any word you got wrong.
f. Word 1. Spell **actively**. Get ready. (Tap for each letter.) *A-C-T-I-V-E-L-Y.*
- (Repeat for: **2. relation, 3. tension, 4. expressive, 5. inactive, 6. marriage.**)

EXERCISE 2

Sentence Variations

a. Get ready to write on lined paper.
- You are going to write a sentence made up of words you know how to spell. Put the right end mark at the end of the sentence.
b. The sentence is: **Several different athletes starred in the show.**
- Say that sentence. Get ready. (Signal.) *Several different athletes starred in the show.*
- (Repeat step *b* until firm.)
c. Write it. ✔
d. Get ready to check your spelling. Put an **X** next to any word you missed.
e. Spell **Several**. Get ready. (Signal.) *S-E-V-E-R-A-L.*
- Check it. ✔
f. Spell **different**. Get ready. (Signal.) *D-I-F-F-E-R-E-N-T.*
- Check it. ✔
- (Repeat step *f* for: **athletes, starred, in, the, show.**)

g. What end mark did you put at the end of the sentence? (Signal.) *A period.*
- Check it. ✔
h. Fix any words you missed.

EXERCISE 3

Prompted Review

a. (Write on the board:)

> 1. station
> 2. surprising
> 3. question
> 4. prolonging
> 5. action
> 6. active

b. Word 1 is **station**. Spell **station**. Get ready. (Signal.) *S-T-A-T-I-O-N.*
c. Word 2 is **surprising**. Spell **surprising**. Get ready. (Signal.) *S-U-R-P-R-I-S-I-N-G.*
d. (Repeat step *c* for: **3. question, 4. prolonging, 5. action, 6. active.**)
e. (Erase the board.)
- Now spell those words without looking.
f. Word 1 is **station**. Spell **station**. Get ready. (Signal.) *S-T-A-T-I-O-N.*
g. Word 2 is **surprising**. Spell **surprising**. Get ready. (Signal.) *S-U-R-P-R-I-S-I-N-G.*
h. (Repeat step *g* for: **3. question, 4. prolonging, 5. action, 6. active.**)
i. (Give individual turns on: **1. station 2. surprising 3. question, 4. prolonging, 5. action, 6. active.**)

LESSON 90

EXERCISE 1

Note: In step e, students will need a red pen (or colored pencil).

Test

a. Today you have a spelling test. Number your lined paper from 1 through 10. ✔
b. Word 1 is **instilled.** What word? (Signal.) *Instilled.*
 • Write the word **instilled.** ✔
c. Word 2 is **breathing.** What word? (Signal.) *Breathing.*
 • Write the word **breathing.** ✔
d. (Repeat step c for: **3. question, 4. cloudiness, 5. straightest, 6. governing, 7. thoughtfully, 8. active, 9. especially, 10. sunniest.**)

e. Pick up your red pen. ✔
 Make an **X** next to any word you spelled wrong.
 • (Write on the board:)

1. instilled	6. governing
2. breathing	7. thoughtfully
3. question	8. active
4. cloudiness	9. especially
5. straightest	10. sunniest

 • Write the correct spelling next to any word you spelled wrong.
 (Observe students and give feedback.)

EXERCISE 1

W as a Vowel Letter

a. You know that if **y** is at the end of a morphograph, then it is a vowel letter.

• The letter **w** is also a vowel letter at the end of a morphograph.

b. Here is the rule for **w:** If **w** is at the end of a morphograph, then it is a vowel letter.

• Listen again: (Repeat the rule.)

c. (Write on the board:)

> 1. show
> 2. drew
> 3. went
> 4. claw
> 5. wonder

d. Number 1 is **show.**

• Is the **w** a vowel letter or a consonant letter in the word **show?** (Signal.) *A vowel letter.*

• How do you know? (Signal.) *It's at the end of a morphograph.*

e. Number 2 is **drew.**

• Is the **w** a vowel letter or a consonant letter in the word **drew?** (Signal.) *A vowel letter.*

• How do you know? (Signal.) *It's at the end of a morphograph.*

f. Number 3 is **went.**

• Is the **w** a vowel letter or a consonant letter in the word **went?** (Signal.) *A consonant letter.*

• How do you know? (Signal.) *It's not at the end of a morphograph.*

g. Number 4 is **claw.**

• Is the **w** a vowel letter or a consonant letter in the word **claw?** (Signal.) *A vowel letter.*

• How do you know? (Signal.) *It's at the end of a morphograph.*

h. Number 5 is **wonder.**

• Is the **w** a vowel letter or a consonant letter in the word **wonder?** (Signal.) *A consonant letter.*

• How do you know? (Signal.) *It's not at the end of a morphograph.*

EXERCISE 2

Word Building

a. (Write on the board:)

> 1. beauty + ful + ly =
> 2. story + es =
> 3. in + act + ive =
> 4. fur + y + est =
> 5. note + ion =
> 6. pro + file =

b. You're going to write the words that go after the equal signs.

• Some of these words follow the final **e** rule. Some follow the doubling rule. Some follow the **y-to-i** rule. Be careful.

• Number your paper from 1 to 6. ✔

c. Word 1: Write **beautifully** on your paper. ✔

d. Do the rest of the words on your own. ✔

e. Check your work. Make an **X** next to any word you got wrong.

f. Word 1. Spell **beautifully.** Get ready. (Tap for each letter.) *B-E-A-U-T-I-F-U-L-L-Y.*

• (Repeat for: **2. stories, 3. inactive, 4. furriest, 5. notion, 6. profile.**)

EXERCISE 3

Spelling Review

a. Get ready to spell and write some words.

b. Word 1 is **station.**

• What word? (Signal.) *Station.*

• Spell **station.** Get ready. (Signal.) *S-T-A-T-I-O-N.*

• Write it. ✔

c. Word 2 is **excited.**

• What word? (Signal.) *Excited.*

• Spell **excited.** Get ready. (Signal.) *E-X-C-I-T-E-D.*

• Write it. ✔

d. (Repeat step c for: **3. nastiness, 4. everyone.**)

e. I'll spell each word.

• Put an **X** next to any word you missed and write that word correctly.

• (Spell each word twice. Write the words on the board as you spell them.)

1. station	3. nastiness
2. excited	4. everyone

EXERCISE 1

Sentence

a. (Write on the board:)

> **Nineteen athletes exercised throughout the morning.**

- I'll read the sentence on the board:
Nineteen athletes exercised throughout the morning.
- Let's spell some of those words.

b. Spell **Nineteen.** Get ready. (Signal.)
N-I-N-E-T-E-E-N.
- Spell **athletes.** Get ready. (Signal.)
A-T-H-L-E-T-E-S.
- Spell **exercised.** Get ready. (Signal.)
E-X-E-R-C-I-S-E-D.
- Spell **throughout.** Get ready. (Signal.)
T-H-R-O-U-G-H-O-U-T.
- Spell **morning.** Get ready. (Signal.)
M-O-R-N-I-N-G.

c. Copy this sentence on lined paper.
(Observe students and give feedback.)

d. Read the sentence you just copied. Get ready. (Signal.) *Nineteen athletes exercised throughout the morning.*

EXERCISE 2

Morphographic Analysis

a. (Write on the board:)

> 1. prolonged = _____
> 2. stylish = _____
> 3. carried = _____
> 4. reactive = _____
> 5. confused = _____
> 6. incurable = _____

- Number your paper from 1 to 6. ✔
- Write the morphographs that go in each blank. Put plus signs between the morphographs. ✔

b. (Write to show:)

> 1. prolonged = pro + long + ed
>
> 2. stylish = style + ish
>
> 3. carried = carry + ed
>
> 4. reactive = re + act + ive
>
> 5. confused = con + fuse + ed
>
> 6. incurable = in + cure + able

c. Check your work. Make an **X** next to any item you got wrong. ✔

EXERCISE 3

Spelling Review

a. You're going to spell words.

b. Word 1 is **recovered.** Spell **recovered.** Get ready. (Signal.) *R-E-C-O-V-E-R-E-D.*

c. Word 2 is **heavier.** Spell **heavier.** Get ready. (Signal.) *H-E-A-V-I-E-R.*

d. Word 3 is **strengthened.** Spell **strengthened.** Get ready. (Signal.) *S-T-R-E-N-G-T-H-E-N-E-D.*

e. Word 4 is **unfriendliest.** Spell **unfriendliest.** Get ready. (Signal.) *U-N-F-R-I-E-N-D-L-I-E-S-T.*

f. Word 5 is **breathe.** Spell **breathe.** Get ready. (Signal.) *B-R-E-A-T-H-E.*

g. Word 6 is **government.** Spell **government.** Get ready. (Signal.) *G-O-V-E-R-N-M-E-N-T.*

h. (Give individual turns on: **1. recovered, 2. heavier, 3. strengthened, 4. unfriendliest, 5. breathe, 6. government.**)

EXERCISE 1

Sentence

a. (Write on the board:)

> **Nineteen athletes exercised throughout the morning.**

- I'll read the sentence on the board: **Nineteen athletes exercised throughout the morning.**
- Let's spell some of those words.

b. Spell **Nineteen.** Get ready. (Signal.) *N-I-N-E-T-E-E-N.*
- Spell **athletes.** Get ready. (Signal.) *A-T-H-L-E-T-E-S.*
- Spell **exercised.** Get ready. (Signal.) *E-X-E-R-C-I-S-E-D.*
- Spell **throughout.** Get ready. (Signal.) *T-H-R-O-U-G-H-O-U-T.*
- Spell **morning.** Get ready. (Signal.) *M-O-R-N-I-N-G.*

c. (Erase the board.)

d. Now let's spell some of the words in that sentence without looking.
- Spell **Nineteen.** Get ready. (Signal.) *N-I-N-E-T-E-E-N.*
- Spell **athletes.** Get ready. (Signal.) *A-T-H-L-E-T-E-S.*
- Spell **exercised.** Get ready. (Signal.) *E-X-E-R-C-I-S-E-D.*
- Spell **throughout.** Get ready. (Signal.) *T-H-R-O-U-G-H-O-U-T.*
- Spell **morning.** Get ready. (Signal.) *M-O-R-N-I-N-G.*

EXERCISE 2

Word Building

a. (Write on the board:)

> 1. quiz + ed =
> 2. show + ing =
> 3. doubt + less =
> 4. stitch + es =
> 5. ex + press + ion =
> 6. in + tent + ion =

b. You're going to write the words that go after the equal signs.
- Some of these words follow the doubling rule. Be careful.
- Number your paper from 1 to 6. ✔

c. Word 1: Write **quizzed** on your paper. ✔

d. Do the rest of the words on your own. ✔

e. Check your work. Make an **X** next to any word you got wrong.

f. Word 1. Spell **quizzed.** Get ready. (Tap for each letter.) *Q-U-I-Z-Z-E-D.*
- (Repeat for: **2. showing, 3. doubtless, 4. stitches, 5. expression, 6. intention.**)

EXERCISE 3

Spelling Review

a. You're going to spell words.

b. Word 1 is **marriage.** Spell **marriage.** Get ready. (Signal.) *M-A-R-R-I-A-G-E.*

c. Word 2 is **answer.** Spell **answer.** Get ready. (Signal.) *A-N-S-W-E-R.*

d. Word 3 is **soundlessly.** Spell **soundlessly.** Get ready. (Signal.) *S-O-U-N-D-L-E-S-S-L-Y.*

e. Word 4 is **hotter.** Spell **hotter.** Get ready. (Signal.) *H-O-T-T-E-R.*

f. Word 5 is **busiest.** Spell **busiest.** Get ready. (Signal.) *B-U-S-I-E-S-T.*

g. Word 6 is **prescribe.** Spell **prescribe.** Get ready. (Signal.) *P-R-E-S-C-R-I-B-E.*

h. (Give individual turns on: **1. marriage, 2. answer, 3. soundlessly, 4. hotter, 5. busiest, 6. prescribe.**)

EXERCISE 1

Sentence

a. (Write on the board:)

> **Nineteen athletes exercised**
> **throughout the morning.**

- I'll read the sentence on the board:
  Nineteen athletes exercised throughout the morning.
- Let's spell some of those words.

b. Spell **Nineteen.** Get ready. (Signal.)
  N-I-N-E-T-E-E-N.
- Spell **athletes.** Get ready. (Signal.)
  A-T-H-L-E-T-E-S.
- Spell **exercised.** Get ready. (Signal.)
  E-X-E-R-C-I-S-E-D.
- Spell **throughout.** Get ready. (Signal.)
  T-H-R-O-U-G-H-O-U-T.
- Spell **morning.** Get ready. (Signal.)
  M-O-R-N-I-N-G.

c. (Erase the board.)

d. Now let's spell some of the words in that sentence without looking.
- Spell **Nineteen.** Get ready. (Signal.)
  N-I-N-E-T-E-E-N.
- Spell **athletes.** Get ready. (Signal.)
  A-T-H-L-E-T-E-S.
- Spell **exercised.** Get ready. (Signal.)
  E-X-E-R-C-I-S-E-D.
- Spell **throughout.** Get ready. (Signal.)
  T-H-R-O-U-G-H-O-U-T.
- Spell **morning.** Get ready. (Signal.)
  M-O-R-N-I-N-G.

EXERCISE 2

Morphographic Analysis

a. (Write on the board:)

> 1. expressive = _____
>
> 2. creative = _____
>
> 3. station = _____
>
> 4. starring = _____
>
> 5. government = _____
>
> 6. signaled = _____

- Number your paper from 1 to 6. ✔
- Write the morphographs that go in each blank. Put plus signs between the morphographs. ✔

b. (Write to show:)

> **1. expressive = ex + press + ive**
>
> **2. creative = create + ive**
>
> **3. station = state + ion**
>
> **4. starring = star + ing**
>
> **5. government = govern + ment**
>
> **6. signaled = sign +al + ed**

c. Check your work. Make an **X** next to any item you got wrong. ✔

Spelling Review

a. You're going to spell words.

b. Word 1 is **doubtlessly.** Spell **doubtlessly.** Get ready. (Signal.) *D-O-U-B-T-L-E-S-S-L-Y.*

c. Word 2 is **furrier.** Spell **furrier.** Get ready. (Signal.) *F-U-R-R-I-E-R.*

d. Word 3 is **actively.** Spell **actively.** Get ready. (Signal.) *A-C-T-I-V-E-L-Y.*

e. Word 4 is **misspending.** Spell **misspending.** Get ready. (Signal.) *M-I-S-S-P-E-N-D-I-N-G.*

f. Word 5 is **sleepiest.** Spell **sleepiest.** Get ready. (Signal.) *S-L-E-E-P-I-E-S-T.*

g. Word 6 is **conserving.** Spell **conserving.** Get ready. (Signal.) *C-O-N-S-E-R-V-I-N-G.*

h. (Give individual turns on: **1. doubtlessly, 2. furrier, 3. actively, 4. misspending, 5. sleepiest, 6. conserving.**)

EXERCISE 1

Sentence

a. You're going to write this sentence:
Nineteen athletes exercised throughout the morning.

b. Say the sentence. Get ready. (Signal.)
Nineteen athletes exercised throughout the morning.

c. Write the sentence. ✔

d. (Write on the board:)

> **Nineteen athletes exercised throughout the morning.**

e. Check your work. Make an **X** next to any word you got wrong. ✔

EXERCISE 2

Word Building

a. (Write on the board:)

> 1. wonder + ful + ly =
> 2. ex + cite + ing =
> 3. pro + found =
> 4. reason + able =
> 5. pause + ing =
> 6. un + stretch + ed =

b. You're going to write the words that go after the equal signs.

• Some of these words follow the final **e** rule. Be careful.

• Number your paper from 1 to 6. ✔

c. Word 1: Write **wonderfully** on your paper. ✔

d. Do the rest of the words on your own. ✔

e. Check your work. Make an **X** next to any word you got wrong.

f. Word 1. Spell **wonderfully**. Get ready. (Tap for each letter.) *W-O-N-D-E-R-F-U-L-L-Y.*

• (Repeat for: **2. exciting, 3. profound, 4. reasonable, 5. pausing, 6. unstretched.**)

EXERCISE 3

Spelling Review

a. You're going to spell words.

b. Word 1 is **station**. Spell **station**. Get ready. (Signal.) *S-T-A-T-I-O-N.*

c. Word 2 is **quizzing**. Spell **quizzing**. Get ready. (Signal.) *Q-U-I-Z-Z-I-N-G.*

d. Word 3 is **notion**. Spell **notion**. Get ready. (Signal.) *N-O-T-I-O-N.*

e. Word 4 is **wrecking**. Spell **wrecking**. Get ready. (Signal.) *W-R-E-C-K-I-N-G.*

f. Word 5 is **thoughtfulness**. Spell **thoughtfulness**. Get ready. (Signal.) *T-H-O-U-G-H-T-F-U-L-N-E-S-S.*

g. Word 6 is **surprise**. Spell **surprise**. Get ready. (Signal.) *S-U-R-P-R-I-S-E.*

h. (Give individual turns on: **1. station, 2. quizzing, 3. notion, 4. wrecking, 5. thoughtfulness, 6. surprise.**)

LESSON 96

EXERCISE 1

Affix Introduction

a. (Write on the board:)

> 1. danger + ous =
> 2. fame + ous =
> 3. joy + ous =

- All these words have the morphograph **o-u-s.**
b. Number your paper from 1 to 3. ✔
c. Add the morphographs together to make new words. Write just the new words. ✔
d. Check your work. Make an **X** next to any word you got wrong.
e. Word 1. Spell **dangerous.** Get ready. (Tap for each letter.) *D-A-N-G-E-R-O-U-S.*
- (Repeat for: **2. famous, 3. joyous.**)

EXERCISE 2

Sentence Variations

a. Get ready to write on lined paper.
- You are going to write a sentence made up of words you know how to spell. Put the right end mark at the end of the sentence.
b. The sentence is: **Nineteen children played actively.**
- Say that sentence. Get ready. (Signal.) *Nineteen children played actively.*
- (Repeat step *b* until firm.)
c. Write it. ✔
d. Get ready to check your spelling. Put an **X** next to any word you missed.
e. Spell **Nineteen.** Get ready. (Signal.) *N-I-N-E-T-E-E-N.*
- Check it. ✔
f. Spell **children.** Get ready. (Signal.) *C-H-I-L-D-R-E-N.*
- Check it. ✔
- (Repeat step *f* for: **played, actively.**)
g. What end mark did you put at the end of the sentence? (Signal.) *A period.*
- Check it. ✔
h. Fix any words you missed.

EXERCISE 3

Prompted Review

a. (Write on the board:)

> 1. throughout
> 2. studious
> 3. questionable
> 4. creatively
> 5. beautiful
> 6. suddenly

b. Word 1 is **throughout.** Spell **throughout.** Get ready. (Signal.) *T-H-R-O-U-G-H-O-U-T.*
c. Word 2 is **studious.** Spell **studious.** Get ready. (Signal.) *S-T-U-D-I-O-U-S.*
d. (Repeat step *c* for: **3. questionable, 4. creatively, 5. beautiful, 6. suddenly.**)
e. (Erase the board.)
- Now spell those words without looking.
f. Word 1 is **throughout.** Spell **throughout.** Get ready. (Signal.) *T-H-R-O-U-G-H-O-U-T.*
g. Word 2 is **studious.** Spell **studious.** Get ready. (Signal.) *S-T-U-D-I-O-U-S.*
h. (Repeat step *g* for: **3. questionable, 4. creatively, 5. beautiful, 6. suddenly.**)
i. (Give individual turns on: **1. throughout, 2. studious, 3. questionable, 4. creatively, 5. beautiful, 6. suddenly.**)

LESSON 97

EXERCISE 1

Word Building

a. (Write on the board:)

> 1. joy + ous =
> 2. un + cover + ed =
> 3. city + es =
> 4. in + act + ive + ly =
> 5. heave + y + ness =
> 6. win + er + s =

b. You're going to write the words that go after the equal signs.
- Some of these words follow the final **e** rule. Some follow the doubling rule. Some follow the **y-to-i** rule. Be careful.
- Number your paper from 1 to 6. ✔
c. Word 1: Write **joyous** on your paper. ✔
d. Do the rest of the words on your own. ✔
e. Check your work. Make an **X** next to any word you got wrong.
f. Word 1. Spell **joyous.** Get ready. (Tap for each letter.) *J-O-Y-O-U-S.*
- (Repeat for: **2. uncovered, 3. cities, 4. inactively, 5. heaviness, 6. winners.**)

EXERCISE 2

Morphographic Analysis

a. (Write on the board:)

> 1. quizzing = _____
>
> 2. joyous = _____
>
> 3. worthiness = _____
>
> 4. refitting = _____
>
> 5. straighten = _____
>
> 6. remarkable = _____

- Number your paper from 1 to 6. ✔
- Write the morphographs that go in each blank. Put plus signs between the morphographs. ✔

b. (Write to show:)

> 1. quizzing = quiz + ing
>
> 2. joyous = joy + ous
>
> 3. worthiness = worth + y + ness
>
> 4. refitting = re + fit + ing
>
> 5. straighten = straight + en
>
> 6. remarkable = re + mark + able

c. Check your work. Make an **X** next to any item you got wrong. ✔

EXERCISE 3

Prompted Review

a. (Write on the board:)

> 1. poisonous
> 2. exercised
> 3. repression
> 4. placement
> 5. relation
> 6. invaluable

b. Word 1 is **poisonous.** Spell **poisonous.** Get ready. (Signal.) *P-O-I-S-O-N-O-U-S.*
c. Word 2 is **exercised.** Spell **exercised.** Get ready. (Signal.) *E-X-E-R-C-I-S-E-D.*
d. (Repeat step *c* for: **3. repression, 4. placement, 5. relation, 6. invaluable.**)
e. (Erase the board.)
- Now spell those words without looking.
f. Word 1 is **poisonous.** Spell **poisonous.** Get ready. (Signal.) *P-O-I-S-O-N-O-U-S.*
g. Word 2 is **exercised.** Spell **exercised.** Get ready. (Signal.) *E-X-E-R-C-I-S-E-D.*
h. (Repeat step *g* for: **3. repression, 4. placement, 5. relation, 6. invaluable.**)
i. (Give individual turns on: **1. poisonous, 2. exercised, 3. repression, 4. placement, 5. relation, 6. invaluable.**)

EXERCISE 1
Word Introduction
a. (Write on the board:)

> scribe
> stove
> fright
> tough
> short
> loose

b. Get ready to read these words.
- First word: **scribe.** What word? (Signal.) *Scribe.*
c. Next word: **stove.** What word? (Signal.) *Stove.*
- (Repeat for: **fright, tough, short, loose.**)
d. Now spell those words.
- Spell **scribe.** Get ready. (Signal.) *S-C-R-I-B-E.*
e. Spell **stove.** Get ready. (Signal.) *S-T-O-V-E.*
- (Repeat for: **fright, tough, short, loose.**)
f. (Erase the board.)
- Spell the words without looking.
g. Spell **scribe.** Get ready. (Signal.) *S-C-R-I-B-E.*
h. Spell **stove.** Get ready. (Signal.) *S-T-O-V-E.*
- (Repeat for: **fright, tough, short, loose.**)

EXERCISE 2
Sentence Variations
a. Get ready to write on lined paper.
- You are going to write a sentence made up of words you know how to spell. Put the right end mark at the end of the sentence.
b. The sentence is: **We worked chiefly throughout the sunny morning.**
- Say that sentence. Get ready. (Signal.) *We worked chiefly throughout the sunny morning.*
- (Repeat step *b* until firm.)
c. Write it. ✔
d. Get ready to check your spelling. Put an **X** next to any word you missed.
e. Spell **We.** Get ready. (Signal.) *W-E.*
- Check it. ✔
f. Spell **worked.** Get ready. (Signal.) *W-O-R-K-E-D.*
- Check it. ✔
- (Repeat step *f* for: **chiefly, throughout, the, sunny, morning.**)
g. What end mark did you put at the end of the sentence? (Signal.) *A period.*
- Check it. ✔
h. Fix any words you missed.

EXERCISE 3
Spelling Review
a. You're going to spell words.
b. Word 1 is **athletes.** Spell **athletes.** Get ready. (Signal.) *A-T-H-L-E-T-E-S.*
c. Word 2 is **carrying.** Spell **carrying.** Get ready. (Signal.) *C-A-R-R-Y-I-N-G.*
d. Word 3 is **reaction.** Spell **reaction.** Get ready. (Signal.) *R-E-A-C-T-I-O-N.*
e. Word 4 is **strengthen.** Spell **strengthen.** Get ready. (Signal.) *S-T-R-E-N-G-T-H-E-N.*
f. Word 5 is **undrinkable.** Spell **undrinkable.** Get ready. (Signal.) *U-N-D-R-I-N-K-A-B-L-E.*
g. Word 6 is **selfishness.** Spell **selfishness.** Get ready. (Signal.) *S-E-L-F-I-S-H-N-E-S-S.*
h. (Give individual turns on: **1. athletes, 2. carrying, 3. reaction, 4. strengthen, 5. undrinkable, 6. selfishness.**)

LESSON 99

EXERCISE 1

Morphographic Analysis

a. (Write on the board:)

> 1. dangerous = _____
>
> 2. station = _____
>
> 3. creative = _____
>
> 4. profiling = _____
>
> 5. suddenly = _____
>
> 6. briefly = _____

- Number your paper from 1 to 6. ✔
- Write the morphographs that go in each blank. Put plus signs between the morphographs. ✔

b. (Write to show:)

> 1. dangerous = danger + ous
>
> 2. station = state + ion
>
> 3. creative = create + ive
>
> 4. profiling = pro + file + ing
>
> 5. suddenly = sudden + ly
>
> 6. briefly = brief + ly

c. Check your work. Make an **X** next to any item you got wrong. ✔

EXERCISE 2

Word Building

a. (Write on the board:)

> 1. pro + cure =
> 2. tough + est =
> 3. un + loose + en =
> 4. re + strict + ion =
> 5. port + ion =
> 6. fame + ous =

b. You're going to write the words that go after the equal signs.
- Some of these words follow the final **e** rule. Be careful.
- Number your paper from 1 to 6. ✔

c. Word 1: Write **procure** on your paper. ✔

d. Do the rest of the words on your own. ✔

e. Check your work. Make an **X** next to any word you got wrong.

f. Word 1. Spell **procure**. Get ready. (Tap for each letter.) *P-R-O-C-U-R-E.*

- (Repeat for: **2. toughest, 3. unloosen, 4. restriction, 5. portion, 6. famous.**)

EXERCISE 3

Prompted Review

a. (Write on the board:)

> 1. extraction
> 2. loosen
> 3. inscribe
> 4. surprising
> 5. storage
> 6. nieces

b. Word 1 is **extraction**. Spell **extraction**. Get ready. (Signal.) *E-X-T-R-A-C-T-I-O-N.*

c. Word 2 is **loosen**. Spell **loosen**. Get ready. (Signal.) *L-O-O-S-E-N.*

d. (Repeat for: **3. inscribe, 4. surprising, 5. storage, 6. nieces.**)

e. (Erase the board.)

Now spell those words without looking.

f. Word 1 is **extraction**. Spell **extraction**. Get ready. (Signal.) *E-X-T-R-A-C-T-I-O-N.*

g. Word 2 is **loosen**. Spell **loosen**. Get ready. (Signal.) *L-O-O-S-E-N.*

h. (Repeat for: **3. inscribe, 4. surprising, 5. storage, 6. nieces.**)

i. (Give individual turns on: **1. extraction, 2. loosen, 3. inscribe, 4. surprising, 5. storage, 6. nieces.**)

Lesson 100

EXERCISE 1

Test

a. Today you have a spelling test. Number your lined paper from 1 through 10. ✔

b. Word 1 is **throughout.** What word? (Signal.) *Throughout.*

- Write the word **throughout.** ✔

c. Word 2 is **dangerous.** What word? (Signal.) *Dangerous.*

- Write the word **dangerous.** ✔

d. (Repeat step *c* for: **3. action, 4. rewrapped, 5. misspelling, 6. babies, 7. uncovered, 8. everyone, 9. unfounded, 10. tensely.**)

e. Pick up your red pen. ✔

- Make an **X** next to any word you spelled wrong.

- (Write on the board:)

1. throughout	6. babies
2. dangerous	7. uncovered
3. action	8. everyone
4. rewrapped	9. unfounded
5. misspelling	10. tensely

- Write the correct spelling next to any word you spelled wrong.
(Observe students and give feedback.)

EXERCISE 1

Word Introduction

a. (Write on the board:)

> script
> tone
> crease
> shrink
> tense
> treat
> seize

b. Get ready to read these words.
- First word: **script.** What word? (Signal.) *Script.*
c. Next word: **tone.** What word? (Signal.) *Tone.*
- (Repeat for: **crease, shrink, tense, treat, seize.**)
d. Now spell those words.
- Spell **script.** Get ready. (Signal.) *S-C-R-I-P-T.*
e. Spell **tone.** Get ready. (Signal.) *T-O-N-E.*
- (Repeat for: **crease, shrink, tense, treat, seize.**)
f. (Erase the board.)
- Spell the words without looking.
g. Spell **script.** Get ready. (Signal.) *S-C-R-I-P-T.*
h. Spell **tone.** Get ready. (Signal.) *T-O-N-E.*
- (Repeat for: **crease, shrink, tense, treat, seize.**)

EXERCISE 2

Word Building

a. (Write on the board:)

> 1. port + ion =
> 2. re + late + ion =
> 3. pro + claim + ed =
> 4. con + sign + ment =
> 5. pre + serve + ing =
> 6. grab + ed =

b. You're going to write the words that go after the equal signs.
- Some of these words follow the final **e** rule. Some follow the doubling rule. Be careful.
- Number your paper from 1 to 6. ✔
c. Word 1: Write **portion** on your paper. ✔
d. Do the rest of the words on your own. ✔
e. Check your work. Make an **X** next to any word you got wrong.
f. Word 1. Spell **portion.** Get ready. (Tap for each letter.) *P-O-R-T-I-O-N.*
- (Repeat for: **2. relation, 3. proclaimed, 4. consignment, 5. preserving, 6. grabbed.**)

EXERCISE 3

Spelling Review

a. You're going to spell words.
b. Word 1 is **unwrap.** Spell **unwrap.** Get ready. (Signal.) *U-N-W-R-A-P.*
c. Word 2 is **children.** Spell **children.** Get ready. (Signal.) *C-H-I-L-D-R-E-N.*
d. Word 3 is **copied.** Spell **copied.** Get ready. (Signal.) *C-O-P-I-E-D.*
e. Word 4 is **wouldn't.** Spell **wouldn't.** Get ready. (Signal.) *W-O-U-L-D-N-'-T.*
f. Word 5 is **profiles.** Spell **profiles.** Get ready. (Signal.) *P-R-O-F-I-L-E-S.*
g. Word 6 is **briefest.** Spell **briefest.** Get ready. (Signal.) *B-R-I-E-F-E-S-T.*
h. (Give individual turns on: **1. unwrap, 2. children, 3. copied, 4. wouldn't, 5. profiles, 6. briefest.**)

LESSON 102

EXERCISE 1

Sentence

a. (Write on the board:)

> **People weren't interested in the photograph.**

- I'll read the sentence on the board: **People weren't interested in the photograph.**
- Let's spell some of those words.
b. Spell **People.** Get ready. (Signal.)
  P-E-O-P-L-E.
- Spell **weren't.** Get ready. (Signal.)
  W-E-R-E-N-'-T.
- Spell **interested.** Get ready. (Signal.)
  I-N-T-E-R-E-S-T-E-D.
- Spell **photograph.** Get ready. (Signal.)
  P-H-O-T-O-G-R-A-P-H.
c. Copy this sentence on lined paper.
  (Observe students and give feedback.)
d. Read the sentence you just copied. Get
  ready. (Signal.) *People weren't interested in
  the photograph.*

EXERCISE 2

Morphographic Analysis

a. (Write on the board:)

> 1. frightened = _____
>
> 2. procure = _____
>
> 3. expressing = _____
>
> 4. throughout = _____
>
> 5. marriage = _____
>
> 6. sunniest = _____

- Number your paper from 1 to 6. ✔
- Write the morphographs that go in
  each blank. Put plus signs between the
  morphographs. ✔

b. (Write to show:)

> 1. frightened = fright + en + ed
>
> 2. procure = pro + cure
>
> 3. expressing = ex + press + ing
>
> 4. throughout = through + out
>
> 5. marriage = marry + age
>
> 6. sunniest = sun + y + est

c. Check your work. Make an **X** next to any
  item you got wrong. ✔

EXERCISE 3

Prompted Review

> *Note:* Use a context sentence for **they're*.**

a. (Write on the board:)

> 1. carrier
> 2. clawed
> 3. placement
> 4. distraction
> 5. they're
> 6. seized

b. Word 1 is **carrier.** Spell **carrier.** Get ready.
  (Signal.) *C-A-R-R-I-E-R.*
c. Word 2 is **clawed.** Spell **clawed.** Get ready.
  (Signal.) *C-L-A-W-E-D.*
d. (Repeat step *c* for: **3. placement,
  4. distraction, 5. they're*, 6. seized.**)
e. (Erase the board.)

- Now spell those words without looking.
f. Word 1 is **carrier.** Spell **carrier.** Get ready.
  (Signal.) *C-A-R-R-I-E-R.*
g. Word 2 is **clawed.** Spell **clawed.** Get ready.
  (Signal.) *C-L-A-W-E-D.*
h. (Repeat step *g* for: **3. placement,
  4. distraction, 5. they're, 6. seized.**)
i. (Give individual turns on: **1. carrier,
  2. clawed, 3. placement, 4. distraction,
  5. they're, 6. seized.**)

EXERCISE 1

Sentence

a. (Write on the board:)

> **People weren't interested in the photograph.**

- I'll read the sentence on the board: **People weren't interested in the photograph.**
- Let's spell some of those words.

b. Spell **People.** Get ready. (Signal.) *P-E-O-P-L-E.*
- Spell **weren't.** Get ready. (Signal.) *W-E-R-E-N-'-T.*
- Spell **interested.** Get ready. (Signal.) *I-N-T-E-R-E-S-T-E-D.*
- Spell **photograph.** Get ready. (Signal.) *P-H-O-T-O-G-R-A-P-H.*

c. (Erase the board.)

d. Now let's spell some of the words in that sentence without looking.
- Spell **People.** Get ready. (Signal.) *P-E-O-P-L-E.*
- Spell **weren't.** Get ready. (Signal.) *W-E-R-E-N-'-T.*
- Spell **interested.** Get ready. (Signal.) *I-N-T-E-R-E-S-T-E-D.*
- Spell **photograph.** Get ready. (Signal.) *P-H-O-T-O-G-R-A-P-H.*

EXERCISE 2

Sentence Variations

a. Get ready to write on lined paper.
- You are going to write a sentence made up of words you know how to spell. Put the right end mark at the end of the sentence.

b. The sentence is: **Our first surprise was beautiful and valuable.**
- Say that sentence. Get ready. (Signal.) *Our first surprise was beautiful and valuable.*
- (Repeat step *b* until firm.)

c. Write it. ✔

d. Get ready to check your spelling. Put an **X** next to any word you missed.

e. Spell **Our.** Get ready. (Signal.) *O-U-R.*
- Check it. ✔

f. Spell **first.** Get ready. (Signal.) *F-I-R-S-T.*
- Check it. ✔
- (Repeat step *f* for: **surprise, was, beautiful, and, valuable.**)

g. What end mark did you put at the end of the sentence? (Signal.) *A period.*
- Check it. ✔

h. Fix any words you missed.

EXERCISE 3

Spelling Review

a. Get ready to spell and write some words.

b. Word 1 is **running.**
- What word? (Signal.) *Running.*
- Spell **running.** Get ready. (Signal.) *R-U-N-N-I-N-G.*
- Write it. ✔

c. Word 2 is **unworthy.**
- What word? (Signal.) *Unworthy.*
- Spell **unworthy.** Get ready. (Signal.) *U-N-W-O-R-T-H-Y.*
- Write it. ✔

d. (Repeat step *c* for: **3. maddest, 4. grief, 5. investment, 6. quoted.**)

e. I'll spell each word.
- Put an **X** next to any word you missed and write that word correctly.
- (Spell each word twice. Write the words on the board as you spell them.)

1. running	4. grief
2. unworthy	5. investment
3. maddest	6. quoted

EXERCISE 1

Sentence

a. (Write on the board:)

> **People weren't interested in the photograph.**

* I'll read the sentence on the board: **People weren't interested in the photograph.**
* Let's spell some of those words.

b. Spell **People.** Get ready. (Signal.) *P-E-O-P-L-E.*
* Spell **weren't.** Get ready. (Signal.) *W-E-R-E-N-'-T.*
* Spell **interested.** Get ready. (Signal.) *I-N-T-E-R-E-S-T-E-D.*
* Spell **photograph.** Get ready. (Signal.) *P-H-O-T-O-G-R-A-P-H.*

c. (Erase the board.)

d. Now let's spell some of the words in that sentence without looking.
* Spell **People.** Get ready. (Signal.) *P-E-O-P-L-E.*
* Spell **weren't.** Get ready. (Signal.) *W-E-R-E-N-'-T.*
* Spell **interested.** Get ready. (Signal.) *I-N-T-E-R-E-S-T-E-D.*
* Spell **photograph.** Get ready. (Signal.) *P-H-O-T-O-G-R-A-P-H.*

EXERCISE 2

Word Building

a. (Write on the board:)

> 1. pre + script + ion =
> 2. tense + ly =
> 3. de + scribe + ing =
> 4. fright + en + ing =
> 5. fame + ous + ly =
> 6. glory + ous =

b. You're going to write the words that go after the equal signs.
* Some of these words follow the final **e** rule. Some follow the **y-to-i** rule. Be careful.
* Number your paper from 1 to 6. ✔

c. Word 1: Write **prescription** on your paper. ✔

d. Do the rest of the words on your own. ✔

e. Check your work. Make an **X** next to any word you got wrong.

f. Word 1. Spell **prescription.** Get ready. (Tap for each letter.) *P-R-E-S-C-R-I-P-T-I-O-N.*
* (Repeat for: **2. tensely, 3. describing, 4. frightening, 5. famously, 6. glorious.**)

EXERCISE 3

Spelling Review

a. Get ready to spell and write some words.

b. Word 1 is **straightest.**
* What word? (Signal.) *Straightest.*
* Spell **straightest.** Get ready. (Signal.) *S-T-R-A-I-G-H-T-E-S-T.*
* Write it. ✔

c. Word 2 is **athlete.**
* What word? (Signal.) *Athlete.*
* Spell **athlete.** Get ready. (Signal.) *A-T-H-L-E-T-E.*
* Write it. ✔

d. (Repeat step c for: **3. nineteen, 4. marrying, 5. question, 6. houseful.**)

e. I'll spell each word.
* Put an **X** next to any word you missed and write that word correctly.
* (Spell each word twice. Write the words on the board as you spell them.)

> | | |
> |---|---|
> | 1. straightest | 4. marrying |
> | 2. athlete | 5. question |
> | 3. nineteen | 6. houseful |

LESSON 105

EXERCISE 1

Sentence

a. You're going to write this sentence: **People weren't interested in the photograph.**

b. Say the sentence. Get ready. (Signal.) *People weren't interested in the photograph.*

c. Write the sentence. ✔

d. (Write on the board:)

> **People weren't interested in the photograph.**

e. Check your work. Make an **X** next to any word you got wrong. ✔

EXERCISE 2

Sentence Variations

a. Get ready to write on lined paper.

• You are going to write a sentence made up of words you know how to spell. Put the right end mark at the end of the sentence.

b. The sentence is: **Was the second question especially maddening?**

• Say that sentence. Get ready. (Signal.) *Was the second question especially maddening?*

• (Repeat step *b* until firm.)

c. Write it. ✔

d. Get ready to check your spelling. Put an **X** next to any word you missed.

e. Spell **Was.** Get ready. (Signal.) *W-A-S.*

• Check it. ✔

f. Spell **the.** Get ready. (Signal.) *T-H-E.*

• Check it. ✔

• (Repeat step *f* for: **second, question, especially, maddening.**)

g. What end mark did you put at the end of the sentence? (Signal.) *A question mark.*

• Check it. ✔

h. Fix any words you missed.

EXERCISE 3

Spelling Review

a. You're going to spell words.

b. Word 1 is **business.** Spell **business.** Get ready. (Signal.) *B-U-S-I-N-E-S-S.*

c. Word 2 is **remarkable.** Spell **remarkable.** Get ready. (Signal.) *R-E-M-A-R-K-A-B-L-E.*

d. Word 3 is **wonderful.** Spell **wonderful.** Get ready. (Signal.) *W-O-N-D-E-R-F-U-L.*

e. Word 4 is **lightness.** Spell **lightness.** Get ready. (Signal.) *L-I-G-H-T-N-E-S-S.*

f. Word 5 is **noisy.** Spell **noisy.** Get ready. (Signal.) *N-O-I-S-Y.*

g. Word 6 is **snapper.** Spell **snapper.** Get ready. (Signal.) *S-N-A-P-P-E-R.*

h. (Give individual turns on: **1. business, 2. remarkable, 3. wonderful, 4. lightness, 5. noisy, 6. snapper.**)

EXERCISE 1

Word Introduction

a. (Write on the board:)

> settle
> argue
> spirit
> thirst
> strict

b. Get ready to read these words.
- First word: **settle.** What word? (Signal.) *Settle.*
c. Next word: **argue.** What word? (Signal.) *Argue.*
- (Repeat for: **spirit, thirst, strict.**)
d. Now spell those words.
- Spell **settle.** Get ready. (Signal.) *S-E-T-T-L-E.*
e. Spell **argue.** Get ready. (Signal.) *A-R-G-U-E.*
- (Repeat for: **spirit, thirst, strict.**)
f. (Erase the board.)
- Spell the words without looking.
g. Spell **settle.** Get ready. (Signal.) *S-E-T-T-L-E.*
h. Spell **argue.** Get ready. (Signal.) *A-R-G-U-E.*
- (Repeat for: **spirit, thirst, strict.**)

EXERCISE 2

Morphographic Analysis

a. (Write on the board:)

> 1. thirsty = _____
>
> 2. restriction = _____
>
> 3. signaling = _____
>
> 4. unreasonable = _____
>
> 5. fitting = _____
>
> 6. denial = _____

- Number your paper from 1 to 6. ✔

- Write the morphographs that go in each blank. Put plus signs between the morphographs. ✔
b. (Write to show:)

> 1. thirsty = thirst + y
>
> 2. restriction = re + strict + ion
>
> 3. signaling = sign + al + ing
>
> 4. unreasonable = un + reason + able
>
> 5. fitting = fit + ing
>
> 6. denial = deny + al

c. Check your work. Make an **X** next to any item you got wrong. ✔

EXERCISE 3

Prompted Review

a. (Write on the board:)

> 1. glorious
> 2. extensive
> 3. first
> 4. toughness
> 5. increase
> 6. package

b. Word 1 is **glorious.** Spell **glorious.** Get ready. (Signal.) *G-L-O-R-I-O-U-S.*
c. Word 2 is **extensive.** Spell **extensive.** Get ready. (Signal.) *E-X-T-E-N-S-I-V-E.*
d. (Repeat step c for: **3. first, 4. toughness, 5. increase, 6. package.**)

e. (Erase the board.)
- Now spell those words without looking.
f. Word 1 is **glorious.** Spell **glorious.** Get ready. (Signal.) *G-L-O-R-I-O-U-S.*
g. Word 2 is **extensive.** Spell **extensive.** Get ready. (Signal.) *E-X-T-E-N-S-I-V-E.*
h. (Repeat for step g: **3. first, 4. toughness, 5. increase, 6. package.**)
i. (Give individual turns on: **1. glorious, 2. extensive, 3. first, 4. toughness, 5. increase, 6. package.**)

LESSON 107

EXERCISE 1

Affix Introduction

a. (Write on the board:)

> **1. press + ure =**
> **2. create + ure =**
> **3. text + ure =**

- All these words have the morphograph **u-r-e.**

b. Number your paper from 1 to 3. ✔

c. Add the morphographs together to make new words. Write just the new words. ✔

d. Check your work. Make an **X** next to any word you got wrong.

e. Word 1. Spell **pressure.** Get ready. (Tap for each letter.) *P-R-E-S-S-U-R-E.*

- (Repeat for: **2. creature, 3. texture.**)

EXERCISE 2

Sentence Variations

a. Get ready to write on lined paper.

- You are going to write a sentence made up of words you know how to spell. Put the right end mark at the end of the sentence.

b. The sentence is: **Some people finished exchanging flowers before everyone else.**

- Say that sentence. Get ready. (Signal.) *Some people finished exchanging flowers before everyone else.*

- (Repeat step *b* until firm.)

c. Write it. ✔

d. Get ready to check your spelling. Put an **X** next to any word you missed.

e. Spell **Some.** Get ready. (Signal.) *S-O-M-E.*

- Check it. ✔

f. Spell **people.** Get ready. (Signal.) *P-E-O-P-L-E.*

- Check it. ✔

- (Repeat step *f* for: **finished, exchanging, flowers, before, everyone, else.**)

g. What end mark did you put at the end of the sentence? (Signal.) *A period.*

- Check it. ✔

h. Fix any words you missed.

EXERCISE 3

Spelling Review

a. You're going to spell words.

b. Word 1 is **valuable.** Spell **valuable.** Get ready. (Signal.) *V-A-L-U-A-B-L-E.*

c. Word 2 is **grabbing.** Spell **grabbing.** Get ready. (Signal.) *G-R-A-B-B-I-N-G.*

d. Word 3 is **friendly.** Spell **friendly.** Get ready. (Signal.) *F-R-I-E-N-D-L-Y.*

e. Word 4 is **cured.** Spell **cured.** Get ready. (Signal.) *C-U-R-E-D.*

f. Word 5 is **different.** Spell **different.** Get ready. (Signal.) *D-I-F-F-E-R-E-N-T.*

g. Word 6 is **flowery.** Spell **flowery.** Get ready. (Signal.) *F-L-O-W-E-R-Y.*

h. (Give individual turns on: **1. valuable, 2. grabbing, 3. friendly, 4. cured, 5. different, 6. flowery.**)

EXERCISE 1

Nonword Base

a. (Write on the board:)

> **1. r e p r e s s i v e**
>
> **2. p r o c l a i m**
>
> **3. d e f o r m i n g**

b. (Point to **repressive**.)
- What word? (Signal.) *Repressive.*
- What's the first morphograph? (Signal.) *Re.*
- Next morphograph? (Signal.) *Press.*
- Next morphograph? (Signal.) *Ive.*

c. Tell me which morphograph in this word could stand alone. (Pause.) Get ready. (Signal.) *Press.*

d. (Point to **proclaim**.)
- What word? (Signal.) *Proclaim.*
- What's the first morphograph? (Signal.) *Pro.*
- Next morphograph? (Signal.) *Claim.*

e. Tell me which morphograph in this word could stand alone. (Pause.) Get ready. (Signal.) *Claim.*

f. (Point to **deforming**.)
- What word? (Signal.) *Deforming.*
- What's the first morphograph? (Signal.) *De.*
- Next morphograph? (Signal.) *Form.*
- Next morphograph? (Signal.) *Ing.*

g. Tell me which morphograph in this word could stand alone. (Pause.) Get ready. (Signal.) *Form.*

h. Some words with more than one morphograph do not contain a morphograph that can stand alone.
- (Erase the morphographs **press, claim,** and **form.** Substitute **cept, gress,** and **tect** to show:)

> **1. r e c e p t i v e**
>
> **2. p r o g r e s s**
>
> **3. d e t e c t i n g**

i. (Point to **receptive**.)
- What word? (Signal.) *Receptive.*
- Tell me what morphograph in this word could stand alone. (Pause.) Get ready. (Signal.) *None of them.*

j. Which morphograph takes the place of a morphograph that could stand alone? (Signal.) *Cept.*
- Spell **cept.** Get ready. (Signal.) *C-E-P-T.*
- Remember, **cept** is a morphograph that cannot stand alone.

k. (Point to **progress**.)
- You can pronounce this word either as **PRO-gress** or **pro-GRESS**.
- None of the morphographs in this word could stand alone.

l. Which morphograph takes the place of a morphograph that could stand alone? (Signal.) *Gress.*
- Spell **gress.** Get ready. (Signal.) *G-R-E-S-S.*
- Remember, **gress** is a morphograph that cannot stand alone.

m. (Point to **detecting**.)
- What word? (Signal.) *Detecting.*
- Tell me what morphograph in this word could stand alone. (Pause.) Get ready. (Signal.) *None of them.*

n. Which morphograph takes the place of a morphograph that could stand alone? (Signal.) *Tect.*
- Spell **tect.** Get ready. (Signal.) *T-E-C-T.*
- Remember, **tect** is a morphograph that cannot stand alone.

o. Get ready to write some words that have the morphographs **cept, gress, and tect.**

p. Word 1: **concept.** Write it. ✔

q. Word 2: **regressing.** Write it. ✔
- (Repeat step *q* for: **3. protect, 4. deceptive.**)

r. I'll spell each word. Put an **X** next to any word you missed and write that word correctly.
- (Spell each word twice. Write the words on the board as you spell them.)

> **1. concept   3. protect**
>
> **2. regressing   4. deceptive**

Word Building

a. (Write on the board:)

> 1. argue + ing =
> 2. re + press + ive =
> 3. tough + ness =
> 4. ex + cite + ing =
> 5. re + tract + ion =
> 6. pre + tense =

b. You're going to write the words that go after the equal signs.
- Some of these words follow the final **e** rule. Be carcful.
- Number your paper from 1 to 6. ✔
c. Word 1: Write **arguing** on your paper. ✔
d. Do the rest of the words on your own. ✔
e. Check your work. Make an **X** next to any word you got wrong.
f. Word 1. Spell **arguing.** Get ready. (Tap for each letter.) *A-R-G-U-I-N-G.*
- (Repeat for: **2. repressive, 3. toughness, 4. exciting, 5. retraction, 6. pretense.**)

Spelling Review

a. You're going to spell words.
b. Word 1 is **photograph.** Spell **photograph.** Get ready. (Signal.) *P-H-O-T-O-G-R-A-P-H.*
c. Word 2 is **treatment.** Spell **treatment.** Get ready. (Signal.) *T-R-E-A-T-M-E-N-T.*
d. Word 3 is **breathing.** Spell **breathing.** Get ready. (Signal.) *B-R-E-A-T-H-I-N-G.*
e. Word 4 is **quickness.** Spell **quickness.** Get ready. (Signal.) *Q-U-I-C-K-N-E-S-S.*
f. Word 5 is **loosen.** Spell **loosen.** Get ready. (Signal.) *L-O-O-S-E-N.*
g. Word 6 is **thrower.** Spell **thrower.** Get ready. (Signal.) *T-H-R-O-W-E-R.*
h. (Give individual turns on: **1. photograph, 2. treatment, 3. breathing, 4. quickness, 5. loosen, 6. thrower.**)

LESSON 109

EXERCISE 1

Nonword Base

a. (Write on the board:)

> **reacting**

b. (Point to **reacting**.)
- What word? (Signal.) *Reacting.*
- What's the first morphograph? (Signal.) *Re.*
- Next morphograph? (Signal.) *Act.*
- Next morphograph? (Signal.) *Ing.*

c. Tell me which morphograph in this word could stand alone. (Pause.) Get ready. (Signal.) *Act.*

d. (Erase the morphograph **act**. Substitute **ject** to show:)

> **rejecting**

e. (Point to **rejecting**.)
- What word? (Signal.) *Rejecting.*
- Tell me what morphograph in this word could stand alone. (Pause.) Get ready. (Signal.) *None of them.*
- Which morphograph takes the place of a morphograph that could stand alone? (Signal.) *Ject.*

f. (Write to show:)

> **rejecting**
>
> **cept**
> **tect**
> **gress**

- Here are three morphographs that cannot stand alone.

g. Spell **cept.** Get ready. (Signal.) *C-E-P-T.*
- (Repeat for **tect** and **gress.**)

h. Listen: **reception.**
- What's the first morphograph? (Signal.) *Re.*
- Next morphograph? (Signal.) *Cept.*
- Next morphograph? (Signal.) *I-O-N.* Yes, I-O-N.
- Spell **reception.** Get ready. (Signal.) *R-E-C-E-P-T-I-O-N.*

i. Listen: **detect.**
- What's the first morphograph? (Signal.) *De.*
- Next morphograph? (Signal.) *Tect.*
- Spell **detect.** Get ready. (Signal.) *D-E-T-E-C-T.*

j. (For **protection [pro + tect + ion], regress [re + gress], detective [de + tect + ive], except [ex + cept], progression [pro + gress + ion],** and **protect [pro + tect],** have students identify each morphograph and spell each word.)

EXERCISE 2

Sentence Variations

a. Get ready to write on lined paper.
- You are going to write a sentence made up of words you know how to spell. Put the right end mark at the end of the sentence.

b. The sentence is: **The yellow flowers won't bloom on the hottest days.**
- Say that sentence. Get ready. (Signal.) *The yellow flowers won't bloom on the hottest days.*
- (Repeat step *b* until firm.)

c. Write it. ✔

d. Get ready to check your spelling. Put an **X** next to any word you missed.

e. Spell **The.** Get ready. (Signal.) *T-H-E.*
- Check it. ✔

f. Spell **yellow.** Get ready. (Signal.) *Y-E-L-L-O-W.*
- Check it. ✔
- (Repeat step *f* for: **flowers, won't, bloom, hottest, days.**)

g. What end mark did you put at the end of the sentence? (Signal.) *A period.*
- Check it. ✔

h. Fix any words you missed.

EXERCISE 3

Spelling Review

a. Get ready to spell and write some words.

b. Word 1 is **descriptive.**

• What word? (Signal.) *Descriptive.*

• Spell **descriptive.** Get ready. (Signal.)
  D-E-S-C-R-I-P-T-I-V-E.

• Write it. ✔

c. Word 2 is **taxes.**

• What word? (Signal.) *Taxes.*

• Spell **taxes.** Get ready. (Signal.) *T-A-X-E-S.*

• Write it. ✔

d. (Repeat step *c* for: **3. action, 4. babyish,
  5. unselfish, 6. playing.**)

e. I'll spell each word.

• Put an **X** next to any word you missed and
  write that word correctly.

• (Spell each word twice. Write the words on
  the board as you spell them.)

1. descriptive	4. babyish
2. taxes	5. unselfish
3. action	6. playing

LESSON 110

EXERCISE 1

> *Note:* In step e, students will need a red pen (or colored pencil).

Test

a. Today you have a spelling test. Number your lined paper from 1 through 10. ✔

b. Word 1 is **photograph.** What word? (Signal.) *Photograph.*

• Write the word **photograph.** ✔

c. Word 2 is **people.** What word? (Signal.) *People.*

• Write the word **people.** ✔

d. (Repeat step *c* for: **3. everyone, 4. weren't, 5. argued, 6. beautiful, 7. denying, 8. flowers, 9. misspell, 10. stories.**)

e. Pick up your red pen. ✔
Make an **X** next to any word you spelled wrong.

• (Write on board:)

1. photograph	6. beautiful
2. people	7. denying
3. everyone	8. flowers
4. weren't	9. misspell
5. argued	10. stories

• Write the correct spelling next to any word you spelled wrong.
(Observe students and give feedback.)

Nonword Base

a. One morphograph that cannot stand alone is **ject.**
   What morphograph? (Signal.) *Ject.*
● Spell **ject.** Get ready. (Signal.) *J-E-C-T.*
b. Get ready to spell words that have the morphograph **ject.**
c. Word 1: **reject.**
   You can pronounce this word either **RE-ject** or **re-JECT.**
● What's the first morphograph in **reject?** (Signal.) *Re.*
● Next morphograph? (Signal.) *Ject.*
● Spell **reject.** Get ready. (Signal.) *R-E-J-E-C-T.*
d. Word 2: **injection.**
● What's the first morphograph in **injection?** (Signal.) *In.*
● Next morphograph? (Signal.) *Ject.*
● Next morphograph? (Signal.) *I-O-N.*
● Spell **injection.** Get ready. (Signal.) *I-N-J-E-C-T-I-O-N.*
e. (For **dejected [de + ject + ed], conjecture [con + ject + ure],** and **project [pro + ject],** have students identify each morphograph and spell each word.)

Word Building

a. (Write on the board:)

> 1. con + cept =
> 2. create + ive =
> 3. un + deny + able =
> 4. tense + ion =
> 5. de + script + ive =
> 6. seize + ure =

b. You're going to write the words that go after the equal signs.
● Some of these words follow the final **e** rule. Some follow the **y-to-i** rule. Be careful.
● Number your paper from 1 to 6. ✔
c. Word 1: Write **concept** on your paper. ✔
d. Do the rest of the words on your own. ✔
e. Check your work. Make an **X** next to any word you got wrong.

f. Word 1. Spell **concept.** Get ready. (Tap for each letter.) *C-O-N-C-E-P-T.*
● (Repeat for: **2. creative, 3. undeniable, 4. tension, 5. descriptive, 6. seizure.**)

Spelling Review

> *Note:* Use a context sentence for **whose*.**

a. Get ready to spell and write some words.
b. Word 1 is **whose*.**
● What word? (Signal.) *Whose.*
● Spell **whose.** Get ready. (Signal.) *W-H-O-S-E.*
● Write it. ✔
c. Word 2 is **sketches.**
● What word? (Signal.) *Sketches.*
● Spell **sketches.** Get ready. (Signal.) *S-K-E-T-C-H-E-S.*
● Write it. ✔
d. (Repeat step *c* for: **3. resign, 4. argue, 5. depression, 6. thirstier.**)
e. I'll spell each word.
● Put an **X** next to any word you missed and write that word correctly.
● (Spell each word twice. Write the words on the board as you spell them.)

1. whose	4. argue
2. sketches	5. depression
3. resign	6. thirstier

EXERCISE 1

Word Introduction

a. (Write on the board:)

> duty
> danger
> round
> speak
> fury
> moist

b. Get ready to read these words.
- First word: **duty.** What word? (Signal.) *Duty.*
c. Next word: **danger.** What word? (Signal.) *Danger.*
- (Repeat for: **round, speak, fury, moist.**)
d. Now spell those words.
- Spell **duty.** Get ready. (Signal.) *D-U-T-Y.*
e. Spell **danger.** Get ready. (Signal.) *D-A-N-G-E-R.*
- (Repeat for: **round, speak, fury, moist.**)
f. (Erase the board.)
- Spell the words without looking.
g. Spell **duty.** Get ready. (Signal.) *D-U-T-Y.*
h. Spell **danger.** Get ready. (Signal.) *D-A-N-G-E-R.*
- (Repeat for: **round, speak, fury, moist.**)

EXERCISE 2

Sentence

a. (Write on the board:)

> Anybody would rather be healthy
> instead of wealthy.

- I'll read the sentence on the board:
Anybody would rather be healthy instead of wealthy.
- Let's spell some of those words.
b. Spell **Anybody.** Get ready. (Signal.) *A-N-Y-B-O-D-Y.*
- Spell **would.** Get ready. (Signal.) *W-O-U-L-D.*
- Spell **rather.** Get ready. (Signal.) *R-A-T-H-E-R.*
- Spell **healthy.** Get ready. (Signal.) *H-E-A-L-T-H-Y.*
- Spell **instead.** Get ready. (Signal.) *I-N-S-T-E-A-D.*
- Spell **wealthy.** Get ready. (Signal.) *W-E-A-L-T-H-Y.*
c. Copy this sentence on lined paper. (Observe students and give feedback.)
d. Read the sentence you just copied. Get ready. (Signal.) *Anybody would rather be healthy instead of wealthy.*

EXERCISE 3

Prompted Review

a. (Write on the board:)

> 1. judged
> 2. greatness
> 3. doubtful
> 4. seizure
> 5. failure
> 6. argued

b. Word 1 is **judged.** Spell **judged.** Get ready. (Signal.) *J-U-D-G-E-D.*
c. Word 2 is **greatness.** Spell **greatness.** Get ready. (Signal.) *G-R-E-A-T-N-E-S-S.*
d. (Repeat for: **3. doubtful, 4. seizure, 5. failure, 6. argued.**)
e. (Erase the board.)
- Now spell those words without looking.
f. Word 1 is **judged.** Spell **judged.** Get ready. (Signal.) *J-U-D-G-E-D.*
g. Word 2 is **greatness.** Spell **greatness.** Get ready. (Signal.) *G-R-E-A-T-N-E-S-S.*
h. (Repeat for: **3. doubtful, 4. seizure, 5. failure, 6. argued.**)
i. (Give individual turns on: **1. judged, 2. greatness, 3. doubtful, 4. seizure, 5. failure, 6. argued.**)

EXERCISE 1

Nonword Base

a. One morphograph that cannot stand alone is **tect.**
   What morphograph? (Signal.) *Tect.*
   • Spell **tect.** Get ready. (Signal.) *T-E-C-T.*
b. Get ready to spell words that have the morphograph **tect.**
c. Word 1: **protect.**
   • What's the first morphograph in **protect?** (Signal.) *Pro.*
   • Next morphograph? (Signal.) *Tect.*
   • Spell **protect.** Get ready. (Signal.) *P-R-O-T-E-C-T.*
d. Word 2: **detect.**
   • What's the first morphograph in **detect?** (Signal.) *De.*
   • Next morphograph? (Signal.) *Tect.*
   • Spell **detect.** Get ready. (Signal.) *D-E-T-E-C-T.*
e. (For **protection [pro + tect + ion]** and **detective [de + tect + ive],** have students identify each morphograph and spell each word.)

EXERCISE 2

Sentence

a. (Write on the board:)

> **Anybody would rather be healthy instead of wealthy.**

   • I'll read the sentence on the board:
   Anybody would rather be healthy instead of wealthy.
   • Let's spell some of those words.
b. Spell **Anybody.** Get ready. (Signal.) *A-N-Y-B-O-D-Y.*
   • Spell **would.** Get ready. (Signal.) *W-O-U-L-D.*
   • Spell **rather.** Get ready. (Signal.) *R-A-T-H-E-R.*
   • Spell **healthy.** Get ready. (Signal.) *H-E-A-L-T-H-Y.*
   • Spell **instead.** Get ready. (Signal.) *I-N-S-T-E-A-D.*
   • Spell **wealthy.** Get ready. (Signal.) *W-E-A-L-T-H-Y.*

c. (Erase the board.)
d. Now let's spell some of the words in that sentence without looking.
   • Spell **Anybody.** Get ready. (Signal.) *A-N-Y-B-O-D-Y.*
   • Spell **would.** Get ready. (Signal.) *W-O-U-L-D.*
   • Spell **rather.** Get ready. (Signal.) *R-A-T-H-E-R.*
   • Spell **healthy.** Get ready. (Signal.) *H-E-A-L-T-H-Y.*
   • Spell **instead.** Get ready. (Signal.) *I-N-S-T-E-A-D.*
   • Spell **wealthy.** Get ready. (Signal.) *W-E-A-L-T-H-Y.*

EXERCISE 3

Spelling Review

a. Get ready to spell and write some words.
b. Word 1 is **excited.**
   • What word? (Signal.) *Excited.*
   • Spell **excited.** Get ready. (Signal.) *E-X-C-I-T-E-D.*
   • Write it. ✔
c. Word 2 is **chiefs.**
   • What word? (Signal.) *Chiefs.*
   • Spell **chiefs.** Get ready. (Signal.) *C-H-I-E-F-S.*
   • Write it. ✔
d. (Repeat step *c* for: **3. duties, 4. thoughtless, 5. couldn't, 6. settlement.**)
e. I'll spell each word.
   • Put an **X** next to any word you missed and write that word correctly.
   • (Spell each word twice. Write the words on the board as you spell them.)

1. excited	4. thoughtless
2. chiefs	5. couldn't
3. duties	6. settlement

EXERCISE 1

Nonword Base

a. One morphograph that cannot stand alone is **gress.**
What morphograph? (Signal.) *Gress.*
- Spell **gress.** Get ready. (Signal.)
G-R-E-S-S.

b. Get ready to spell words that have the morphograph **gress.**

c. Word 1: **progress.**
You can pronounce this word either **PRO-gress** or **pro-GRESS.**
- What's the first morphograph in **progress?** (Signal.) *Pro.*
- Next morphograph? (Signal.) *Gress.*
- Spell **progress.** Get ready. (Signal.)
P-R-O-G-R-E-S-S.

d. Word 2: **progressive.**
- What's the first morphograph in **progressive?** (Signal.) *Pro.*
- Next morphograph? (Signal.) *Gress.*
- Next morphograph? (Signal.) *Ive.*
- Spell **progressive.** Get ready. (Signal.)
P-R-O-G-R-E-S-S-I-V-E.

e. (For **regress [re + gress]** and **progression [pro + gress + ion],** have students identify each morphograph and spell each word.)

EXERCISE 2

Sentence

a. (Write on the board:)

> **Anybody would rather be healthy instead of wealthy.**

- I'll read the sentence on the board:
Anybody would rather be healthy instead of wealthy.
- Let's spell some of those words.

b. Spell **Anybody.** Get ready. (Signal.)
A-N-Y-B-O-D-Y.
- Spell **would.** Get ready. (Signal.)
W-O-U-L-D.
- Spell **rather.** Get ready. (Signal.)
R-A-T-H-E-R.
- Spell **healthy.** Get ready. (Signal.)
H-E-A-L-T-H-Y.

- Spell **instead.** Get ready. (Signal.)
I-N-S-T-E-A-D.
- Spell **wealthy.** Get ready. (Signal.)
W-E-A-L-T-H-Y.

c. (Erase the board.)

d. Now let's spell some of the words in that sentence without looking.
- Spell **Anybody.** Get ready. (Signal.)
A-N-Y-B-O-D-Y.
- Spell **would.** Get ready. (Signal.)
W-O-U-L-D.
- Spell **rather.** Get ready. (Signal.)
R-A-T-H-E-R.
- Spell **healthy.** Get ready. (Signal.)
H-E-A-L-T-H-Y.
- Spell **instead.** Get ready. (Signal.)
I-N-S-T-E-A-D.
- Spell **wealthy.** Get ready. (Signal.)
W-E-A-L-T-H-Y.

EXERCISE 3

Spelling Review

a. Get ready to spell and write some words.

b. Word 1 is **children.**
- What word? (Signal.) *Children.*
- Spell **children.** Get ready. (Signal.)
C-H-I-L-D-R-E-N.
- Write it. ✔

c. Word 2 is **detection.**
- What word? (Signal.) *Detection.*
- Spell **detection.** Get ready. (Signal.)
D-E-T-E-C-T-I-O-N.
- Write it. ✔

d. (Repeat step c for: **3. pressure, 4. hopping, 5. rejection, 6. unrounded.**)

e. I'll spell each word.
- Put an **X** next to any word you missed and write that word correctly.
- (Spell each word twice. Write the words on the board as you spell them.)

1. children	4. hopping
2. detection	5. rejection
3. pressure	6. unrounded

LESSON 115

EXERCISE 1

Nonword Base

> *Note:* Use a context sentence for **except***.

a. One morphograph that cannot stand alone is **cept.**
   What morphograph? (Signal.) *Cept.*
- Spell **cept.** Get ready. (Signal.) *C-E-P-T.*
b. Get ready to spell words that have the morphograph **cept.**
c. Word 1: **concept.**
- What's the first morphograph in **concept?** (Signal.) *Con.*
- Next morphograph? (Signal.) *Cept.*
- Spell **concept.** Get ready. (Signal.) *C-O-N-C-E-P-T.*
d. Word 2: **except*.**
- What's the first morphograph in **except?** (Signal.) *Ex.*
- Next morphograph? (Signal.) *Cept.*
- Spell **except.** Get ready. (Signal.) *E-X-C-E-P-T.*
e. (For **receptive [re + cept + ive]** and **deception [de + cept + ion],** have students identify each morphograph and spell each word.)

EXERCISE 2

Sentence

a. You're going to write this sentence:
   Anybody would rather be healthy instead of wealthy.
b. Say the sentence. Get ready. (Signal.) *Anybody would rather be healthy instead of wealthy.*
c. Write the sentence. ✔
d. (Write on the board:)

> **Anybody would rather be healthy instead of wealthy.**

e. Check your work. Make an **X** next to any word you got wrong. ✔

EXERCISE 3

Prompted Review

a. (Write on the board:)

> **1. knowing**
> **2. unhealthy**
> **3. surely**
> **4. creature**
> **5. closure**
> **6. pressure**

b. Word 1 is **knowing.** Spell **knowing.** Get ready. (Signal.) *K-N-O-W-I-N-G.*
c. Word 2 is **unhealthy.** Spell **unhealthy.** Get ready. (Signal.) *U-N-H-E-A-L-T-H-Y.*
d. (Repeat for: **3. surely, 4. creature, 5. closure, 6. pressure.**)
e. (Erase the board.)
- Now spell those words without looking.
f. Word 1 is **knowing.** Spell **knowing.** Get ready. (Signal.) *K-N-O-W-I-N-G.*
g. Word 2 is **unhealthy.** Spell **unhealthy.** Get ready. (Signal.) *U-N-H-E-A-L-T-H-Y.*
h. (Repeat for: **3. surely, 4. creature, 5. closure, 6. pressure.**)
i. (Give individual turns on: **1. knowing, 2. unhealthy, 3. surely, 4. creature, 5. closure, 6. pressure.**)

EXERCISE 1

Morphographic Analysis

a.   (Write on the board:)

> 1. protection = _____
>
> 2. detective = _____
>
> 3. progression = _____
>
> 4. reception = _____
>
> 5. moisture = _____
>
> 6. increase = _____

- Number your paper from 1 to 6. ✔
- Write the morphographs that go in each blank. Put plus signs between the morphographs. ✔

b.   (Write to show:)

> 1. protection = pro + tect + ion
>
> 2. detective = de + tect + ive
>
> 3. progression = pro + gress + ion
>
> 4. reception = re + cept + ion
>
> 5. moisture = moist + ure
>
> 6. increase = in + crease

c.   Check your work. Make an **X** next to any item you got wrong. ✔

EXERCISE 2

Sentence Variations

a.   Get ready to write on lined paper.
- You are going to write a sentence made up of words you know how to spell. Put the right end mark at the end of the sentence.

b.   The sentence is: **Wouldn't anybody rather have strength than weakness?**
- Say that sentence. Get ready. (Signal.) *Wouldn't anybody rather have strength than weakness?*
- (Repeat step *b* until firm.)

c.   Write it. ✔

d.   Get ready to check your spelling. Put an **X** next to any word you missed.

e.   Spell **Wouldn't.** Get ready. (Signal.) *W-O-U-L-D-N-'-T.*
- Check it. ✔

f.   Spell **anybody.** Get ready. (Signal.) *A-N-Y-B-O-D-Y.*
- Check it. ✔
- (Repeat step *f* for: **rather, have, strength, than, weakness.**)

g.   What end mark did you put at the end of the sentence? (Signal.) *A question mark.*
- Check it. ✔

h.   Fix any words you missed.

EXERCISE 3

Spelling Review

> *Note:* Use context sentences for **they're*** and **it's***.

a.   You're going to spell words.

b.   Word 1 is **unworthy.** Spell **unworthy.** Get ready. (Signal.) *U-N-W-O-R-T-H-Y.*

c.   Word 2 is **scripture.** Spell **scripture.** Get ready. (Signal.) *S-C-R-I-P-T-U-R-E.*

d.   Word 3 is **inform.** Spell **inform.** Get ready. (Signal.) *I-N-F-O-R-M.*

e.   Word 4 is **increasing.** Spell **increasing.** Get ready. (Signal.) *I-N-C-R-E-A-S-I-N-G.*

f.   Word 5 is **they're*.** Spell **they're.** Get ready. (Signal.) *T-H-E-Y-'-R-E.*

g.   Word 6 is **it's*.** Spell **it's.** Get ready. (Signal.) *I-T-'-S.*

h.   (Give individual turns on: **1. unworthy, 2. scripture, 3. inform, 4. increasing, 5. they're, 6. it's.**)

EXERCISE 1

Word Building

a. (Write on the board:)

> 1. in + tense + ive =
> 2. re + strict + ion =
> 3. skin + ed =
> 4. risk + y + ness =
> 5. vent + ure =
> 6. humor + ous =

b. You're going to write the words that go after the equal signs.
- Some of these words follow the final **e** rule. Some follow the doubling rule. Some follow the **y-to-i rule.** Be careful.
- Number your paper from 1 to 6. ✔
c. Word 1: Write **intensive** on your paper. ✔
d. Do the rest of the words on your own. ✔
e. Check your work. Make an **X** next to any word you got wrong.
f. Word 1. Spell **intensive.** Get ready. (Tap for each letter.) *I-N-T-E-N-S-I-V-E.*
- (Repeat for: **2. restriction, 3. skinned, 4. riskiness, 5. venture, 6. humorous.**)

EXERCISE 2

Sentence Variations

a. Get ready to write on lined paper.
- You are going to write a sentence made up of words you know how to spell. Put the right end mark at the end of the sentence.
b. The sentence is: **It was sunny throughout the glorious day.**
- Say that sentence. Get ready. (Signal.) *It was sunny throughout the glorious day.*
- (Repeat step *b* until firm.)
c. Write it. ✔
d. Get ready to check your spelling. Put an **X** next to any word you missed.
e. Spell **It.** Get ready. (Signal.) *I-T.*
- Check it. ✔
f. Spell **was.** Get ready. (Signal.) *W-A-S.*
- Check it. ✔
- (Repeat step *f* for: **sunny, throughout, the, glorious, day.**)

g. What end mark did you put at the end of the sentence? (Signal.) *A period.*
- Check it. ✔
h. Fix any words you missed.

EXERCISE 3

Prompted Review

> *Note:* Use a context sentence for **except***.

a. (Write on the board:)

> 1. except
> 2. dangerous
> 3. proportion
> 4. reception
> 5. moisture
> 6. quizzes

b. Word 1 is **except***. Spell **except.** Get ready. (Signal.) *E-X-C-E-P-T.*
c. Word 2 is **dangerous.** Spell **dangerous.** Get ready. (Signal.) *D-A-N-G-E-R-O-U-S.*
d. (Repeat step *c* for: **3. proportion, 4. reception, 5. moisture, 6. quizzes.**)
e. (Erase the board.)
- Now spell those words without looking.
f. Word 1 is **except***. Spell **except.** Get ready. (Signal.) *E-X-C-E-P-T.*
g. Word 2 is **dangerous.** Spell **dangerous.** Get ready. (Signal.) *D-A-N-G-E-R-O-U-S.*
h. (Repeat step *g* for: **3. proportion, 4. reception, 5. moisture, 6. quizzes.**)
i. (Give individual turns on: **1. except, 2. dangerous, 3. proportion, 4. reception, 5. moisture, 6. quizzes.**)

EXERCISE 1

Morphographic Analysis

a. (Write on the board:)

> 1. treatment = _____
>
> 2. progressive = _____
>
> 3. creation = _____
>
> 4. joyous = _____
>
> 5. confusing = _____
>
> 6. moodiness = _____

- Number your paper from 1 to 6. ✔
- Write the morphographs that go in each blank. Put plus signs between the morphographs. ✔

b. (Write to show:)

> 1. treatment = treat + ment
>
> 2. progressive = pro + gress + ive
>
> 3. creation = create + ion
>
> 4. joyous = joy + ous
>
> 5. confusing = con + fuse + ing
>
> 6. moodiness = mood + y + ness

c. Check your work. Make an **X** next to any item you got wrong. ✔

EXERCISE 2

Sentence Variations

a. Get ready to write on lined paper.
- You are going to write a sentence made up of words you know how to spell. Put the right end mark at the end of the sentence.

b. The sentence is: **A famous and wealthy man was interested in the photograph.**
- Say that sentence. Get ready. (Signal.) *A famous and wealthy man was interested in the photograph.*
- (Repeat step *b* until firm.)

c. Write it. ✔

d. Get ready to check your spelling. Put an **X** next to any word you missed.

e. The first word is **A.**
- Check it. ✔

f. Spell **famous.** Get ready. (Signal.) *F-A-M-O-U-S.*
- Check it. ✔
- (Repeat step *f* for: **and, wealthy, man, was, interested, in, the, photograph.**)

g. What end mark did you put at the end of the sentence? (Signal.) *A period.*
- Check it. ✔

h. Fix any words you missed.

EXERCISE 3

Spelling Review

a. You're going to spell words.

b. Word 1 is **marrying.** Spell **marrying.** Get ready. (Signal.) *M-A-R-R-Y-I-N-G.*

c. Word 2 is **thief.** Spell **thief.** Get ready. (Signal.) *T-H-I-E-F.*

d. Word 3 is **passive.** Spell **passive.** Get ready. (Signal.) *P-A-S-S-I-V-E.*

e. Word 4 is **beauty.** Spell **beauty.** Get ready. (Signal.) *B-E-A-U-T-Y.*

f. Word 5 is **watching.** Spell **watching.** Get ready. (Signal.) *W-A-T-C-H-I-N-G.*

g. Word 6 is **rained.** Spell **rained.** Get ready. (Signal.) *R-A-I-N-E-D.*

h. (Give individual turns on: **1. marrying, 2. thief, 3. passive, 4. beauty, 5. watching, 6. rained.**)

EXERCISE 1

Word Building

a. (Write on the board:)

> 1. fury + ous =
> 2. in + tense + ly =
> 3. special + ly =
> 4. re + late + ive =
> 5. un + reason + able =
> 6. de + tect + ion =

b. You're going to write the words that go after the equal signs.
- Some of these words follow the final **e** rule. Some follow the **y-to-i** rule. Be careful.
- Number your paper from 1 to 6. ✔
c. Word 1: Write **furious** on your paper. ✔
d. Do the rest of the words on your own. ✔
e. Check your work. Make an **X** next to any word you got wrong.
f. Word 1. Spell **furious**. Get ready. (Tap for each letter.) *F-U-R-I-O-U-S.*
- (Repeat for: **2. intensely, 3. specially, 4. relative, 5. unreasonable, 6. detection.**)

EXERCISE 2

Sentence Variations

a. Get ready to write on lined paper.
- You are going to write a sentence made up of words you know how to spell. Put the right end mark at the end of the sentence.
b. The sentence is: **A fanciful surprise excited the thoughtful children.**
- Say that sentence. Get ready. (Signal.) *A fanciful surprise excited the thoughtful children.*
- (Repeat step *b* until firm.)
c. Write it. ✔
d. Get ready to check your spelling. Put an **X** next to any word you missed.
e. The first word is **A.** Get ready for article "A".
- Check it. ✔
f. Spell **fanciful.** Get ready. (Signal.) *F-A-N-C-I-F-U-L.*
- Check it. ✔
- (Repeat step *f* for: **surprise, excited, the, thoughtful, children.**)
g. What end mark did you put at the end of the sentence? (Signal.) *A period.*
- Check it. ✔
h. Fix any words you missed.

EXERCISE 3

Spelling Review

a. You're going to spell words.
b. Word 1 is **inventive.** Spell **inventive.** Get ready. (Signal.) *I-N-V-E-N-T-I-V-E.*
c. Word 2 is **another.** Spell **another.** Get ready. (Signal.) *A-N-O-T-H-E-R.*
d. Word 3 is **confuse.** Spell **confuse.** Get ready. (Signal.) *C-O-N-F-U-S-E.*
e. Word 4 is **package.** Spell **package.** Get ready. (Signal.) *P-A-C-K-A-G-E.*
f. Word 5 is **straighten.** Spell **straighten.** Get ready. (Signal.) *S-T-R-A-I-G-H-T-E-N.*
g. Word 6 is **progression.** Spell **progression.** Get ready. (Signal.) *P-R-O-G-R-E-S-S-I-O-N.*
h. (Give individual turns on: **1. inventive, 2. another, 3. confuse, 4. package, 5. straighten, 6. progression.**)

LESSON 120

EXERCISE 1

> *Note:* In step e, students will need a red pen
> (or colored pencil).

Test

a. Today you have a spelling test. Number
   your lined paper from 1 through 10. ✔

b. Word 1 is **government.** What word?
   (Signal.) *Government.*

• Write the word **government.** ✔

c. Word 2 is **marriage.** What word? (Signal.)
   Marriage.

• Write the word **marriage.** ✔

d. (Repeat step c for: **3. spinning,
   4. signaling, 5. especially,
   6. unreasonable, 7. protective,
   8. hopelessness, 9. different,
   10. voltage.**)

e. Pick up your red pen. ✔
   Make an **X** next to any word you spelled
   wrong.

• (Write on the board:)

1. government	6. unreasonable
2. marriage	7. protective
3. spinning	8. hopelessness
4. signaling	9. different
5. especially	10. voltage

• Write the correct spelling next to any word
  you spelled wrong.
  (Observe students and give feedback.)